Wolverhampton
voices

SAINT PETERS
CHURCH
WOLVERHAMPTON

Tempus ORAL HISTORY *Series*

Wolverhampton
voices

Alec Brew

TEMPUS

Frontispiece St Peter's Church, the focal point of Wolverhampton for a thousand years, though most of the building is far more recent.

First published 2004

Tempus Publishing Limited
The Mill, Brimscombe Port,
Stroud, Gloucestershire, GL5 2QG

© Alec Brew, 2004

British Library Cataloguing in Publication Data.
A catalogue record for this book is available from the British Library.

ISBN 0 7524 3283 4

Typesetting and origination by Tempus Publishing Limited
Printed in Great Britain

Contents

The Conservatory in West Park, one of the finest Victorian Parks in the country.

Acknowledgements

As well as the contributors, who downloaded their memory banks for me, I should also like to thank Harry Blewitt and David Clare for some of the photographs, and all the other people I have spoken to over the years; even if your memories are not to be found here, you have helped to paint a picture of this wonderful old town and helped me to find my way around its living history.

Introduction

'Change and decay in all around I see.' Nostalgia is a funny thing: people look back to days when everything was so much harder but claim that they were so much happier then. No one can deny that things have changed since the days when lodgers slept four to a room, two in a bed, or when baths were taken in front of the fire, or when 'faggots and pays' were the very best of meals, but were people happier then? This book tries to preserve people's memories of Wolverhampton – what it was like at home, at school or at work, the good times and the bad.

While compiling books on Wolverhampton, I have been only too well aware that many of the hundreds of people I have talked to have had stories to tell which could not be included, because they had no photographs to accompany them. This book is a chance to set down some of those memories, to turn oral history into written history.

It is clear that in living memory Wolverhampton has changed almost beyond recognition, not least from a town to a city. The older generation remember a life lead in close-knit neighbourhoods of terraced houses, with front doors opening onto the street; outside, often communal, toilets; and large families squashed into a few rooms. Mothers took in washing or did a bit of cleaning to make ends meet. Fathers worked in the local large companies such as Chillington Tool in Horseley Fields, Bayliss, Jones & Bayliss in Monmore Green, Stafford Road Works or ECC in Bushbury, Butlers in Springfield, or Joseph Evans in Heath Town. They worked with iron and steel, coming home exhausted and blackened from their toil, and their sons expected nothing more than to follow in their footsteps.

Their recreation was playing football or bowls and drinking a pint or two of 'Spring' or 'Banks mild' in the local with a game of dominoes. Watching the Wolves was both pleasure and pain, and a visit to East or West Park was a special treat. Kids played hopscotch in the street or swam in the canal. If they got up to mischief their teacher or the local bobby gave them a clip round the ear, and if they complained to their parents they got another one. People barely strayed from their own neighbourhood; they had everything they wanted right there, even their own local cinema. Going into town was a rarity, even though it was only walking distance away.

How things have changed in the twenty-first century. Most of those large industrial companies have gone, Goodyear being the latest casualty. People work in smaller, far more varied companies, and they rarely walk to work any more, they drive in from the leafy suburbs after dropping their children off at school. There has been more change in the last fifty years than the 200 before that. Kids today think 'The War' is ancient history, if they even know which war you mean. Computer games have replaced hopscotch, gaming machines have replaced dominoes, but watching the Wolves is still a mixture of pleasure and pain.

Recording people's memories is vital if the children of the twenty-first century are ever to discover what it was like in the good/bad old days (delete the word you think appropriate). A way of life is disappearing fast, and photographs only preserve split seconds. A volume such as this can only record a small measure of Wulfrunians' memories, but I hope that even if your life's recollections are not recorded, there will be someone else's just like them.

Although I have largely used peoples own words to describe their experiences, I have edited their stories into some sort of sensible order. Many of the people I spoke to had broad Wolverhampton accents – music to my ears – and I was tempted to try and reproduce the Black Country words and phrases phonetically. Reason prevailed in the end, when I realised that many readers 'woe spake proper English like wot us do' so I have kept only a small taste of the idiosyncrasies of the local accent. I hope that people reading the resulting sentences will not be offended by my alterations in the direction of 'Oxford English', or embarrassed by the local spelling and grammar which remains. 'If it dow sound loik yow, its cos them from Brummagem and beyond cor unnerstand rale English loik wot way spake.'

one

At Home

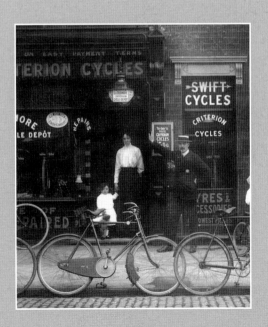

Detail of Dugmore's cycle shop, 253-257 Bilston Road, around 1908.

Lodgings in South Street

When I went to work in Oxley Sidings in 1910, I lodged in one of the houses in South Street. It was by an entry on the bend, a typical terraced house with a front room, a back room and a scullery, with three bedrooms. The family that lived there had three daughters, Harriet, Georgie and Alice, and a son named Harry, who had lost a nut or two. There were two other lodgers, Charlie Jones and George Meredith.

The mother and father had one bedroom, the three daughters the next, and the three lodgers shared the front bedroom with the son, Harry. There were only two beds, me sharing one with Charlie, and George sharing with Harry. Harry used to have vivid dreams and he used to cling to George in the night with a tight grip. George used to wake up shouting 'Loose, you bloody thing!' hitting Harry to make him let go.

We were just three country lads away from home for the first time and we used to fool around a lot, pillow fights, knocking all the knick-knacks off the mantelpiece and such. The daughters used to play jokes on us, putting holly in our beds or sewing lace round the bottom of our trousers.

The eldest, Harriet, was a midwife; she was learning her midwifery at the hospital. The other, Georgie, was a typist or something, and she was courting a miner from the other side of Bridgnorth. The youngest, Alice, was the stop-at-home, cook the meals etc. type. You never used to see the mother until dinnertime.

Well we got in the front room one night, and Harry was tinkling on the piano. Charlie got the nurse, I think, George had got Georgie,

James Daniel Brew, aged sixteen, just before he went to work in Oxley Sidings.

cos she'd fell for him, and I'd got Alice, and we turned the gas lamps out. We kept Harry tinkling on the piano to hide the bother. By God, along from the kitchen comes mother, she opened the door and found the place in darkness, and did she lay the law down: 'I won't have such disgraceful carry-ons in my house!'

Dan Brew, born 1892

Bilston Road

I was born Maud Charlotte Violeta Poole in 1906, and we lived on the Bilston Road, just beyond the railway bridges in Monmore Green. The house was just beyond the Monmore Green School. We lived in a back house, and there was a long passage which lead from a house where another family lived next to the Bilston Road, Mr and Mrs Betts, who never had any children. I had two brothers, but I was the only girl. My mother did a bit of cleaning, and my father worked in Adam's, right at the top of Ettingshall Lane where the canal is; it was a big ironworking place. There was another similar place opposite, Holcroft's. My father was what they called a packer; he used to pack the scrap iron to put into the furnace. He worked there as long as I can remember. He always used to say, 'I shall have a better job, or I shall have nare a one.' I used to take him his supper, a twopenny pork chop he used to have off the Green.

Where the Victoria pub is now on the Bilston Road, next to it there used to be a chapel, which I used to go to. Every year we had an anniversary parade, all the chapels did, and all the children used to dress up and we used to parade round the streets with a little band, and stop every now and then to sing off the hymn sheets. Well I have a picture of me in my anniversary dress. It used to go in the pawn shop when we were short of money.

Where the greyhound track is now there used to be what we called the water engine, a great big wheel in a deep pool, but alongside that there used to a steep incline down to a flat part, and the girls used to run down that, straight into a chap's arms. I used to like that. Beyond that there was a sailor who got drowned. There was a square pool near the Willenhall Road and he went in to save someone and he got drowned. He was buried at St Matthew's Church in Horseley Fields.

We used to have a tin bath in the house, in front of the fire. But many's the time I've had a bath in the washing boiler in the yard, because it had a fire under it. My father never went in a pub, but he liked a drink, and so did me Mom. He used to go up town, and what he really liked was when they had the Salvation Army band round the statue in Snow Hill. They had a Sunday morning there, with the music, and he loved that. My mother couldn't go because she couldn't walk, with the arthritis. Dad used to have a walk out Saturday night, and he would come back with the *War Illustrated*, not the *War Cry*, because it had more pictures, rather than stories. I remember having a bath on the hearth, and I would sit there and wait for him to come back, and I would read the Illustrated sitting in the bath.

I left school when I was fourteen. I went to work in a toy factory, Hobran's, for about eighteen months, making little toy steam engines, but I was finished after Christmas when the trade fell off. The factory was where Steelways is now. I hung around for a couple of weeks, and then my Mom found me a job in Monmore Green in service with Lewis the butcher. I was there for about twenty-five years. He [Lewis] had four children; his wife died and I more or less brought them up, but I really grew up with the children because I was only about sixteen myself. Before that

Above The funeral of Harry Parks Temple, the sailor who drowned trying to save two children in a pool off Stow Heath Lane. Outside St Matthew's Church, Horseley Fields.

Right Ethel Bradney and Blanche Price outside Price's shop at 143 Bilston Road.

I used to take the papers round for Mrs Parkes, who was beyond the bridges. I think she gave me half a crown a week, but I didn't see it, it went to my mother. I only had a bit of pocket money off my father, twopence, to spend on sweets or whatever.

Across the road from Lewis the butcher was St Silas's Church, and just below, about six shops down, was Mr Lewis' brother, Enoch, who used to work in the abattoir which was by the cattle market, not far away. The cows used to come up the road and over the bridge with a drover, and it was just as if they could

Dugmore's cycle shop, 253-257 Bilston Road, around 1908. Note the tram tracks in the road, a constant danger to cyclists.

smell it, the abattoir: they used to run every-where. Down in the Green, in one of the back houses, there was a family called the Beamons, and they had a piano, which was unusual. One day they'd left their front door open and a cow who had escaped came in and left its calling card across the piano. Another day one came down our entry off the Bilston Road and it left milk all over the floor. The cows were full of milk, desperate to be milked. The kids used to take a bucket to where the cows were crying up the cattle market and milk them in the dirty bucket. I had a bike, and I used to bike from Lewis' down to where we lived, and I was always frightened to death I would meet the cattle being driven up the road to the market.

I really enjoyed life then. Monmore Green was a little town on its own, there was every-thing you needed: three butchers' shops, a paper-hanging shop, a chemist, post office, two or three grocers, Mr Dawes, Mr Simpson and Mr Whitmore. Then coming over the canal bridge was a chap as used to mend shoes; then we had three pubs on that side of the road, the Oddfellows, the Barrel and the Black Horse, then there was the Bush and the Lion, and the British Oak on the other side. In Chapel Square was the Woodman. There was a pawn shop opposite the abattoir, and a coal wharf (Mrs Evans's), and there was another wharf up Cable Street. There was everything on the Green; there was no need to go to town. I never went to town when I was a kid.

Mr and Mrs Betts, who lived in the house in front of ours, had her sister come from Warrington, and they had two boys, and they took me to the West Park with them for a treat; I thought I was in a foreign country!

Lewis' had a cart and a horse, and four could sit in this trap, two at the back and two at the front, and we used to go out in this trap to Kingswood; it was like going abroad. We went there many a time, like on Thursday afternoon, when he shut the shop.

The family moved up to York Street about 1938, when those houses were new, and I've lived here ever since; that really was in Monmore Green.

Maude Law (née Poole), born 1906

Darlington Street

I was born in Lower Stafford Street in the Royal Hussar Pub, opposite the Elephant and Castle. My father died when I was two and a half and left mother a widow, with the three of us, and then the family split up; the grand-parents had us and that. Then we went to live in Darlington Street: it was a three-storey pub, a very nice house, on the edge of Townwell Fold, which went down to Beatties. When mother first went there it was called the Hole in the Wall, then it was changed soon after to the Joiners Arms; she was the licensee for Butler's Brewery.

I went to St Peter's School. I used to go across Darlington Street, up through the Fold there, by the Town Hall, then up Cheapside, and across the terrace to the school; my sister and I went together. When I was in the infants, Miss Jones was the headmistress, then I went into the higher school, and the head-mistress was Miss Hewins.

When I left school I went to the British School of Commerce to study shorthand typing, and that used to be over what was

The Royal Hussar pub in Lower Stafford Street with landlord, Sam Evans, and his wife Mary, their son Samuel, and their daughter Mary.

called the Empire, in the Labour Rooms, in Queen Square where there was the Hippodrome, and the Labour Rooms were next to it. You used to go up some stairs and I learned shorthand typing there. I had a year's job in an office, but I didn't like it and I went into a shop.

Clara Williams, born 1911

Springfield

I was born at 36 Grimstone Street, Springfield, opposite Butler's Brewery offices. They had a clock, which used to chime every quarter of an hour. In the night, I was never a very good sleeper, I just lay and listened to it strike the quarter and half hour. Mostly it

The wedding of Alfred and Edna Hill in Jones Road, 1940, looking towards Wolverhampton Gas Works. Edna Bradley, sister of the groom, is third from the left in the back row.

was a poor area. There were thirteen of us in our family; I was the fourth. It was a two–up and two–down house. We used to sleep four in a bed, two at one end and two the other. We had candlelight and went up the stairs with a candle.

I had to do my share of the chores. When I was twelve years old I had to do a day's washing when mother was confined. There was a high tub and a boiler, and you had to light the boiler and use a large mangle. I used to peg out the washing in a big yard at the back, and there was lines all across it.

The footbridge over the low-level railway used to be called the 'Nineteen Steps', but there never were nineteen steps, there was only eighteen. Us children used to count them up and count them down, and it was always the same question: 'Where's the nineteenth step?' A little further on under the

high-level railway bridge and on the canal side was a mission hall called Barge Mission, used mostly by the boat people moored there and in the 'A' Basin in Broad Street. My best friend and I used to go every Sunday evening. In the winter there would be a big blazing open fire and we sang hymns at the top of our voices. Happy days.

I used to play by the canal, running over the lock gates. When my son did that later, I smacked his legs. In the street we played tip-cat and tops.

My father worked at Butler's Brewery in the cooperage for fifty years. His name was William Luke Hill, but he was known in Springfield as Bill Hill.

I remember May Day; the horses used to be decorated with ribbons and paraded through the town. Butler's used to take us children out on the drays for a day out in the country, at Coven, for games and a picnic. We had lots of good, clean fun. It was lovely.

There was a chip shop just below us in Grimstone Street for many years, but there was another in Bridge Street, what is now Culwell Street, by the Nineteen Steps, kept by a Japanese couple, the Watabikis. They came just after the First World War. They had a hard time getting started but they were quite a nice family. I always went in there for a penny's worth of chips, and a penny fish.

On holidays we also used to go to West Park and to Tettenhall on the Green. We used to pay a penny on the tram. For a halfpenny you could get two pounds of Tettenhall pears – Tettenhall Dicks we used to call them. On Saturdays we used to go to the Olympia, which was in Thornley Street, and we used to pay one penny to go in there, and for that they also used to give you a bag of sweets. We used to go and sit on the front row. It was silent films, Charlie Chaplin and that, and a cousin of mine, whose name was Manlove, played the piano at the Olympia.

When I was very tiny my Grandfather used to take me to the Pavilion in Tower Street. It now belongs to the Express and Star. They did half revues and half pictures. He used to take me Friday evening in the Gods. When we came out of there he used to pop out to the Wheatsheaf pub and leave me in the yard.

Elsie Bradley, born 1908

Monmore Green

I've lived in Monmore Green all my life. My Granny, Granny Mayer, had a shop on the Green and she used to sell everything, even lamp oil. They used to say on the Green, 'Get your lamp oil from Granny Mayer, 'erll give you sum suck'. I used to like pulling the lever up and down until you'd got the measurement to fill their can. They [customers] would never use to come until they would start to light the lamps up, just as you were having your tea. I used to have a cousin named Lizzie, what lived with me Gran, and Auntie Ginnie and Uncle Charlie, and she used to go mad because after you'd sold the lamp oil you had got to go and wash your hands again to get the oil off, before going back to your tea.

My Gran used to sell firewood; the man used to bring it all chopped and tied in bundles. She used to go up the market and buy oranges and bananas, the green ones, and hang them up from the ceiling. She used to have tins of sweets in the window and I loved to fill the tins up with sweets, and I don't think my Granny ever let me have a sweet, and I never used to take one either.

Granny Mayer outside her shop in Monmore Green, with her daughter Betty just visible in the window.

My Gran used to like a half-pint of beer. There were two houses next to her shop, then a bakehouse, and then a little outdoor pub owned by Hipkisses. Me Gran used to like her half-a-pint during the day, and she would keep it in a jug on a shelf in the shop, and she would have a little sip now and then. Sometimes she would have a bit more and she would say either Mrs Hipkiss or Miss Hipkiss had been in a good mood and given her 'the long pull'.

If anyone came in the shop and wanted to start talking about someone, Gran used to say 'Now ma wench, tha know the short answer, what they do is their business, an' I dow want to know nothing about it.' She didn't want gossip in her shop.

Next to my Granny's shop was a pawn shop. I don't know the man's name who owned the pawn shop because he owned one or two. The people used to come with bundles of clothes to pawn and Gran used to give them a ticket and throw the bundle on the floor, and I used to go round the pawn shop to help her to stack them. They used to do all the washing, fold it all up and then pawn it until the weekend, when they would go and fetch it out again. Their Sunday suit would go in the pawn. Two shops past Baker Street was Jimmy Price's butchers' shop. It was known as Jimmy Duck's because he used to sell faggots, which were known as 'ducks'.

Over the road from Granny Mayer's shop, my Mom's Auntie Becky Chance opened her front room and used to make roly-poly fruit and that for the workers at dinnertime, and they used to queue up outside. Next door was a second-hand shop owned by Mr Hammond, who was an inspector on the buses. When the bus company had the sales of the lost property that had not been claimed, he would buy it and sell it in the shop, and of course the factory people used to come in for the odd gloves to work in, to prevent the cold and stop a lot of cuts to their fingers.

Old Nell, who kept the second-hand clothes shop, used to buy rabbit skins off people and then take them to the skin market on Bilston Road. I can't remember if it was twopence or threepence she bought them for, and then she would sell them for sixpence.

There was a rat-catcher on the Green named Norman Evans, who had a little terrier dog called Barney, and on a Sunday afternoon there would be a crowd of people in a great big ring in the square outside the Woodman. He used to loose the rat, and he'd have Barney between his legs, and then he'd loose Barney, who would have the rat in no time. Barney would give it one shake and bring it straight back to his master. The men used to bet on it. At other times he used to let the ferret out instead of Barney, and that was the sort of entertainment we had on a Sunday afternoon.

The rat-catcher's mother kept a shop in the square, a greengrocer, and she was also a moneylender. If people borrowed half a crown, they had to pay back an extra sixpence. They couldn't see it but eventually they were borrowing their own money.

There used to be bookmakers, taking bets on horses. They used to stand on the corners taking bets. There was a man named Mr Simpson and, when he was taking bets, if the policeman, whose name was Darnley, used to come, someone would shout a warning and Simpson would drop his bets and he'd be off up one entry and down the other. Even if they caught him, he had nothing on him to show he'd been taking bets. He was caught once when this policeman came along in a wheelchair. Someone came pushing this wheelchair, and when they came by the entry, he jumped out, and that was the time he did nab Simpson, with the bets on him.

An outing setting off from the Woodman, Chapel Square, Monmore Green. This is the square where rat-catching was a spectator sport.

I went to Monmore Green School, but I didn't have a lot of schooling because I was an epileptic. I would be away for a few days and then when I went back I'd be all worked up about missing the lessons, so I'd be off again. That's why I was always up me Gran's shop all the while, and helping in the pawn shop too.

Lily Garbitt (*née* Mayer), born 1920

Monmore Green

My family lived in Miner Street, Monmore Green. There was Mom and Dad and seven girls in a two–bedroom house. The girls slept six to a bed, top and bottom. We were very poor. My father was gassed during the war and didn't have a job most of the time, so Mom took in washing every day to give us one good meal a day. She worked six days a week, but on holidays from school we all went to the East Park for the day. Dinnertime one of us would go home to get crab apples and ginger pop or water.

I went to Monmore Green School and remember Mr Lindley, the headmaster, and Mr Simcox, a lovely man, but who used to throw the blackboard duster at you if he thought you weren't listening.

We had no money but those days were the best days of my life really; my sisters and I are always talking about Monmore Green. Life was happy then even though we were poor. I remember the men standing at the top of the yard (not many men had jobs) sharing a cigarette. I was twelve when we left but I shall always remember lots of lovely times.

Mrs D. Beckett (*née* Ellis), born 1927

Edward and Caroline Smith with their children, Dorothy and Norman. Mr Smith ran a furniture business in Ettingshall, and had made the pedal tricycle.

Catchem's Corner, Ettingshall

I lived in Catchem's Corner for sixty-five years. The area was enclosed between the two canals and the two railway bridges, mostly taken up by John Thompson's boiler works, where I worked. In that small area there were forty-one houses and two pubs, the Bull's Head, on the corner, and the Mill. There was also a post office and several shops which were actually part of the houses. You could buy everything you wanted there. We hardly ever came into contact with other communities. Us kids were used to playing with kids from other areas, but not as adults.

My father, Edward Smith, ran a furniture business in Ettingshall. He had a horse named

Betty which used to pull the cart which delivered the furniture. My brother Norman, sister Dorothy and I had a pedal cycle made like a horse and cart. One of us sat on the horse and pedalled and the other sat in the cart behind.

The area was called Catchem's Corner and there are two versions of how it got its name. The corner is actually the junction of Millfields Road and Ettinghshall Road, which used to be called Hell Lane, a notorious by-way where robbers lurked in Victorian times. One story was that the police used to lurk on the corner to 'catch 'em', and the other concerned a thief, a foot-pad named Riley or something like that. His nickname was Old Catchem, and apparently he used to hide in the bushes around there before robbing people. He bought a bit of land in John Street, Ettingshall, with his ill-gotten gains and for some reason gave it to the local Methodists, who had prayed and prayed for a bit of land, and became a pillar of the Church.

There was a lot of open ground around Lanesfield, where I went to school, and the children would be out there playing. The houses had outside toilets in the back garden then. The council used to come and empty them at night, but they weren't too particular where they put the contents, and waste ground would do, and they would throw ashes over it. It looked like solid ground, but it was actually up to five feet deep in hollows. I've seen one or two go up to their necks. You had to know your ground pretty well round there!

Catchem's Corner is unrecognisable now; John Thompson's is all gone, though the buildings are still there, and the house where I was born is still standing, but it's called Pete's Cafe now. My mother ran the cafe for a while. She used to open at 5.00 in the morning and close at 10.00 at night. And she made her own ice cream.

Lawrence Smith, born 1922

Portland Place, All Saints

Next to the Royal Hospital was the street where I was born, Portland Place (next to Sutherland Place) in 1938. At the very top of our street was no. 22; I lived in no. 21. When I was about five years old, the hospital decided to build a new X-ray department, and offered my family a house at no. 18, which was infested with bugs and fleas, so my mother refused. Eventually the hospital renovated this house and we moved in. The people at no. 22 left the area, the two houses were demolished and the department was built. About five years later the hospital took the whole street for their car park, and we bought a house in Rugby Street. Portland Place no longer existed.

Mercy K. Jackson, born 1938

Shaw Road, Bushbury

I was born in Shaw Road, Bushbury. We lived at what was, before they renumbered the houses, no. 2 Ivy Bank, Shaw Road, which was five houses with an entry between them. There were nine of us: eight brothers and Ivy, our sister. The brothers were Arthur, Cyril, Horace, Ted, Frank, Griff, Harry (me) and Jack. It was a three-bedroom house, with two beds in each room. There was three in a bed sometimes.

I went to Bushbury Lane School, what is now Oxley primary, and to Old Fallings School for a while, which previously was a girls' school, then I went to Bushbury Hill. I then went to evening classes at Dunkerley Street, three nights a week. I took an electrical course at the Tech. We were the first to attend the Technical College, actually, and my first teacher was Dr Fisher, who taught us maths. That was 1934-35, and I completed the course and had a certificate in electrical science.

In those days there was nothing on the one side of Stafford Road at all. It was Staveley Hill's estate at Oxley Manor. He bought cows in Canada and transferred them from Oxley Sidings over a bridge, so the cows could walk right on to his estate. His house was a beautiful big house; I have been all through it. They've knocked it down of course. It was at the bottom of Ribbesford Avenue. The farmhouse became the Homestead pub. They had to blast the cowsheds to demolish them because they were concrete.

There were two elephants kept in a big corrugated, round-roofed shed at Dunstall Park, and they used to come by every week. Salt

Above Bushbury Lane School, who had beaten Prestwood Road School 3-1 at Molineux in 1928. Harry Jones is fourth from the left in the front row. Isiah Foley was the headmaster, and Mr Lowe the teacher.

Right The Homestead pub as it currently appears, though it used to be a farmhouse.

and Susie they were called. They also had little ponies which used to waddle round the elephants' legs. On the bend in Shaw Road there was an allotments, and my Dad put some cabbages just over the fence and the elephants ate his cabbages.

Harry Jones, born 1917

Whitmore Reans

I was born in Upper Gornal, where my mother came from, but we moved to Lloyd Street, Whitmore Reans, when I was six months old. My mother was in service, and she used to work in pubs. She used to start at 4.00 or 5.00 in the morning, because the pubs were open all day before the First World War. The man she was in service with, Mr Lamb, took over the Summerhouse on the corner of Lloyd Street, Whitmore Reans, so we moved there. Later on he took over the Criterion Hotel, on Prince's Square.

My father came from Derby. He worked as a painter at The Sunbeam and applied the fine lines and details. I still have his line brushes in the garage, he looked after them. I also have some gold leaf he used to do the shop signs for F.W. Woolworth's, applying the gold leaf to the letters.

I went to St Jude's junior school, which had an orphanage on the opposite corner, in St Jude's Road. They were both Church-financed of course. Afterwards I went to Hordern Road Senior School. Hordern Road is now St Andrew's junior and infants; that school moved down from where it used to be above the other side of the old St Andrew's Church. The playing fields for Hordern Road were down by the canal, where Giffard Primary School is now.

The Methodist church had a large array of buildings behind, a church hall and that, and the boys' brigade used to meet there. On a Sunday morning they would decide to wake

An aerial view of West Park, with the Territorial Army drill hall top left. The horses were ridden around the park for exercise.

The Wolverhampton yeomanry emerging from the drill hall, which is now gone, apart from the façade.

the neighbourhood up at around 10.00 a.m., out marching round with their drums. Whitmore Reans was a lovely close community in those days. Everyone seemed to know everyone else and they all got on.

The local trolleybuses were 2 or 2A, one going down Newhampton Road, along Court Road and back up Horden Road, and the other going the other way round. One day, when I was about four or five, my Dad said we were going to look at the trams. Now there had not been any trams in Wolverhampton for years. My Dad had a bicycle with a seat on the back where I could sit, and we cycled out to the Wergs, and down Wergs Hall Road. There was a field between Wergs Hall and the road, and it was full of trams. That was where they put them when they were retired. I was very impressed.

I remember the old urinal in Leicester Square. It was a cast-iron circular thing, and it was said that the cast iron had corroded away and the local scrap man put in a bid to take it away. Something else I remember was an emergency police bell on a pole at the top of Coleman Street. There was a red box on a pole with a glass face, and you smashed the glass to ring the bell and the police would come from Red Lion Street or Dunstall Road.

The Territorial Army Riding School which was next to West Park has recently been turned into flats. West Park was surrounded by a ten- or twelve-foot-wide grass verge, and that was used to exercise the horses, which used to ride around and around the park. The bollards were not there in front of the gates then, so the horses could go by. I remember seeing that in the 1920s and '30s.

Whitmore Reans is not the same now.

Bill Pauling, born 1927

Park Village

I was born in Park Village, above a second-hand shop, a lock-up shop, next to Lorings the bakers. My father worked in Chillington Tool, in charge of the hardening shop. I can remember going there as a kid during the war, and there was this great pile of hand grenade cases. They'd been sent in for annealing, so they broke up when they exploded.

The schools I went to were all in Park Village. The first was St Faith's infants' school on the corner of Park Lane, then I went up Woden Road, to the junior school, and then I went a bit further up to Springfield Road School.

George Brazier, born 1927

Walsall Street

I was born in Shrubbery Street, just off Walsall Street. Lots of people never knew the place existed. Next to the British Oxygen place, between there and the railway bridges, was the little Shrubbery Street estate of terraced houses. There was a yard at the back and the toilets were at the bottom of the yard, four toilets for all the families. You would be in the dark walking down the yard to the toilets. We only had the old gas lights. Next to the toilets was the brew house where you did your washing, and everyone had their day to do their washing. There was a big boiler and underneath was a little fire. In the morning you would light the fire to heat the water to do your washing. Shrubbery Street is not there any more, British Oxygen knocked it all down and expanded up to the railways a long time ago.

In 1938, when I was eight, we moved from Shrubbery Street to Ashbourne Road.

When I was in the Army, doing my National Service, I was on fourteen days' embarkation leave, waiting to go to Fayid in Egypt. I came home and we went camping to Bridgnorth. We went on the bus, it was 2s 3d return. We kept fowl, and everyday me Dad biked all the way home to feed the fowl. On the Friday he came back and said that I had a telegram and that I had to report back to Whittington Barracks the following morning,

because they wanted me on the permanent staff. I used to play football and box, and they wanted me on the teams.

Doug Quinton, born 1930

Moseley Road

I was born in Moseley Road and I went to Moseley Village School, where Deansfield High School is now. There was a little church next door, St Matthias, then a junior school, then the infants and a few houses. There was a jungle gym in the infants, and a climbing frame which I loved, but when we went to the juniors we couldn't go on it any more. I didn't want to leave the infants for that reason. It was on concrete as well, none of this soft stuff to land on which they have these days.

Down Moseley Road was what we called the Potted Meat Place. It was actually called the Butchers Hide and Skin, which faced on to where I lived, across a field where they used to keep horses. Mr Grosvenor owned the field, and he used to cut it for hay as well. Beyond that was another little field where they used to have the bonfires on 5 November. Some of the lads used to get the barrels that had held the fat from over the road in the Potted Meat Place, and they used to burn well.

There was a pool which ran to the road, and then another pool, and then a field, and the sewage from the works used to run in three channels into that field. Cows' horns and horses' hooves used to come out, and the dog used to bring them home. I think they abstracted something to do with soap from them. The fishermen used to get the maggots from there as well. The smell was awful. If the wind was blowing in the wrong direction, you could smell it as far as Monmore Green. Our hobby was killing the big meat flies on the wall of the house. You used to get a big rolled up newspaper and see who could kill the most.

Florence Quinton (née Roberts) born 1934

Above The VE Day 'street party' at the top of Lawnswood Rise, Blakeley Green.

Right Mrs Jeggering in Blakeley Avenue, Claregate, during the war, having fled there with her husband and sons. Mr Jeggering served in the Princess Irene Brigade of the Dutch Army at Wrottesley Park.

Blakeley Green

We came to Blakeley Avenue at the outbreak of war. We had just got married on 12 August 1939 and we were looking for houses. We couldn't get a mortgage because I was military age, so we had to rent this house; it was nineteen and six a week. When we finally bought it, it was £700. Originally, when it was new it was £495. We bought it in 1943 or 1944, while I was still in the Navy. We had £70 in the post office which we had to use as a deposit, and Betty had a devil of a job getting post to me to get the money out, as it was in my name.

When we first came here some of the houses were not finished, and not a lot of them were sold. A lot of RAF people from RAF Cosford were renting the houses. Of course it was all open at the back then, and the children used to play up there. It was open at the back until after the war, when they built the houses in Lawnswood Avenue. At the end of the war, the VE Day party was held there at the top of Lawnswood Rise. The tables were even laid out in a V shape.

During the war a Dutch family rented the house next door at no. 21, Mrs Jeggering and her husband and their two sons, Tony and Ronnie. They had fled from the Germans and Mr Jeggering had joined the Dutch Army, which was based at Wrottesley Park. The boys went to school at St Andrew's in Whitmore Reans. Mrs Jeggering used to keep hens in the back garden and she sometimes gave me an egg. I used to grow vegetables so I used to give her vegetables, if we had any.

They used to occasionally hear from their parents, who were farmers, during the war. Apparently they lost everything. When they returned to Holland all the neighbours were trying to gather things together for them to take with them. They didn't settle in Holland, they came back to East Anglia and started a smallholding, before going to Canada.

Percy Kyte, born 1916

Coventry Street

I was born Leah Pritchard on a small farm in Jones Field at the back of Coventry Street, off the Willenhall Road, in 1925. My family lived at no. 54 Coventry Street, where I grew up.

Each Friday I was given one penny pocket money, and the time I spent at the shop window agonising over the choice of sweets was half pleasure and half pain. There were boxes of all different kinds: there was dab and suckers, lucky bags, cream pies, gobstoppers, chops, peas and potatoes, locust beans, liquorice Catherine wheels, bootlaces and pipes, and jars of kali in different colours. I can

see it now in tall glass jars standing among the boxes of sweets in the window.

I would buy a ha'penny worth of red kali and a ha'penny worth of yellow kali, and I would take it home and make pop with it. Then I would fill two bottles and my friend and I would take it with the sandwiches that my mother had made for us and we would set off for East Park for a picnic. We had to cross the Willenhall Road to get to the park, but I do not remember an adult ever having to see us across the road. It was a main road but there was hardly any traffic on it; few people owned cars.

What pleasures we children enjoyed in the pre-television days. Life revolved around street games such as skipping, top and whip, kick the can, or swimming at Heath Town swimming baths. There was also Sunday school at the Bethel Chapel and each year we would go for a day's outing; there would be a prize for good attendance. We also had a Christmas Party and every child had a present off the Christmas tree.

On Saturday afternoons we would go to the Globe Cinema in Horseley Fields or the Olympia off Broad Street for the matinee. Both these cinemas were called the fleapits, though I never knew why.

Lizzie Pritchard under her cherry tree at 54 Coventry Street with her daughters Lily, Leah and Minnie, and Minnie's sons Brian and Alan.

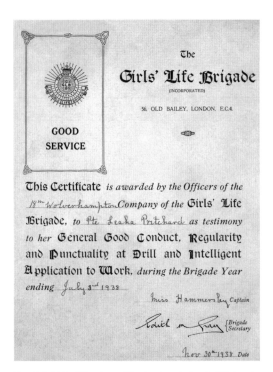

The Girls' Life Brigade certificate given to Leah Pritchard at the Bethel Chapel, Horseley Fields.

The wedding of Jack Freeman and Lily Pritchard at 54 Coventry Street during the war.

When I was old enough I joined the Girls' Life Brigade at the Bethel Chapel, and my parents made sure they could send me camping with the brigade each year. My Dad would take me to the railway station where we all had to meet, and as he kissed me goodbye he would put his hand in his pocket and place a shilling in my hand to add to the small amount of pocket money I had. I had many a holiday in Wales this way, but I never had a holiday with my parents. Most of their money went on paying the mortgage on their house, and to own your own home in those days was an achievement, as most homes were rented.

Four of us from our Life Brigade also went to the Maypole Dance at the Albert Hall in London. We had pretty little dresses made, and more people came from other Life Brigade chapels.

When my sister, Lily, got married just before the war, she got married in a Catholic church in Bilston, because Jack Freeman, her husband, was a Catholic. We had the photographs for her wedding taken in the garden in Coventry Street. My father was still alive then, but he wasn't when I got married.

Monday in our house was wash day. I often wondered why it had to be Monday, why not Tuesday or Wednesday? My mother would be up at dawn. First she would fill the copper with water, light the fire underneath and then wash all the whites, and then put them in the copper to boil. Then she would relax for five minutes to have a quick breakfast. Breakfast was one slice of toast and a cup of tea. After this short break she would wash the coloureds, wring them through the heavy mangle, which I was often asked to turn, and then hang them out on the clothes line. Then a kettle of water had to be boiled to make the starch to stiffen the table clothes, aprons and collars. After a sandwich for lunch she would be ironing, which took all afternoon. If it rained there was such a panic to get all the washing off the line and to hang it on a clothes horse round the fire. How lucky we are today with washing machines, dryers and clothes that don't need much ironing.

Leah Brew (*née* Pritchard), born 1925

'The Dirty Five' of Steelhouse Lane. From left to right, back row: Harold Broadfield, George Rowley and James Owen. Front: Sid Allan and Noah Williams.

Eagle Street

Our family lived in Eagle Street, which was just round the corner from Monmore Green, and I had many friends down there. In fact I was one of the few people to be allowed to walk down there unmolested. It was a very close community, and even policemen were not accepted down there, that is until Jerry O'Leary came to Wolverhampton Police Force in the 1920s. I can still see him walking down the street in my memory: tall, slim and ginger-haired. When he first came to the town he was sent on a bike down to the Green, and I suppose all the coppers were laughing their heads off. Jerry was promptly thrown in the Cut. He climbed out bringing his bike with him and rode right down the Green and back again. So, although he had a soaking he had the last laugh at the station, because he was accepted by the Greenites.

I was accepted in the Green because our uncle, Ted Owen, lived there. He was known as Stopper, because he was a goalkeeper, and I think he played for the Wolves. Another close friend of mine down there was Billy Reynolds, of the professional boxing family. Another uncle of mine, James, was also a goalkeeper; he played for Merthyr Tydfil in Wales. He was one of five blokes who all lived down Steelhouse Lane and were related by marriage. They were known as The Dirty Five, for some reason. There was Uncle Jim and Harold Broadfield, who served in the Leeds/West Yorkshire Regiment during the First World War, and Sid Allan who was gassed in the trenches with the 6th South Staffords. There was also George Rowley, who was the cousin of Arthur Rowley, the all-time top scorer in the football league. He went to Dudley Road School, as did his brother Jack, who later played for Manchester United.

Noah Williams' Morgan sports car at the back of his shop in Blakhalve Lane.

The last one of The Dirty Five was Noah Williams, who opened a shop in the Rough Hills and which became the first of a chain. He did well for himself and I remember he later owned a Morgan sports car.

All Saints and Monmore Green schools were great rivals at football and cricket. I played in both of those games. Monmore Green played on a pitch on East Park.

Ben Owen, born 1923

Great Brickkiln Street

There were a great many characters in the old days. For instance, Old Stan, who used to live in, and reputedly owned most of, Ashland Street, off Great Brickkiln Street, was a character who always wore an old mac and had a great hooked nose, a bit like Desperate Dan from the comics. You would always find him at 4.00 p.m. outside the convent on St John Street, Snow Hill, queuing with the others for his meal and pocket money, distributed daily by the nuns.

I remember lining up at the gates of the coal yard, top of Shepherd Street, off Brickkiln Street, to rush the gates when the owner got there, to grab a truck just to take home 1 cwt of coal weekly. Otherwise it meant following the successful collector around until such time as they had finished with their truck, often all morning. The yard closed about 12 noon Saturday, so no truck, no coal, no fires for a week! But grabbed early I could deliver the others and earn a fortune, threepence for a morning's work.

I remember the old mission huts on Compton Road where, as a child, I had to collect, with coupons, National Dried Milk for my younger brother, which I later collected from Beatties on a Saturday.

I remember the Pat Collins Fair and the circus held at the top of Brickkiln Street adjoining Peel Street. Kids used to grub around after their departure looking for dropped coins, as indeed they did when the old market shut for the day. I also remember collecting boxes and making up bundles of firewood to sell, along with another well-known character, 'Singing Margaret'.

I remember being lookout for bookies' runners and taking bets to local greengrocers for my father, money and slip always wrapped up in newspaper: 'Wait until the shop is empty' was the instruction.

There were good dishonest people and almost saintly people who made up the streets of the old town.

Arthur Maker

Stafford Street

I was born in Stafford Street. My parents had a shop, double fronted; on the one side my mother, Lillian, kept a grocery, and on the other my father, Joseph Henry Price, kept cycle parts, and at one time he had the biggest trade in car tyres in Wolverhampton. Next door to us was a lodgings and next door to that was a garage. In 1932 the chap who owned the garage bought the whole block and we had to move out. My father heard that the

Bill Price, landlord of the Colonel Vernon, North Street, who reputedly could fell a shire horse with a single blow.

Warwick Arms on the corner of Littles Lane and St Mary's Terrace was open for tenancy, so that's where we went. My Grandfather, Bill Price, who had been in the Army during the Boer War, had kept the Colonel Vernon in North Street, though he now had the Prince of Wales in Middle Row. At one time he also had the Blue Bull on the Bilston Road, near the cattle market.

To start with, me and my sister, Sylvia, shared a room on the second floor, but when we got older she kept that room and I moved into a room on the top floor. We had a maid at that time and she also had a room on the top floor. We went to St Peter's School. The pub's clientele was largely Irish, because it was in the Irish Quarter. We did a very good trade on 17 March, St Patrick's Day. There are no houses there now, of course; the ring road did away with all those. At that time Carver's was at the top of Stafford Street, a smallish place.

When my uncle Horace got married they had a wedding photograph took in the blacksmith's yard opposite the Colonel Vernon. It was rented to Percy Bates, who lived in Camp Street. He was the last blacksmith working in Wolverhampton. Uncle Horace later took over the Duke of York in Market Street, it's the Tap 'n' Spile now. After he left that he took over the Swan with Two Necks in Pool Street, opposite the Sunbeamland. Another uncle, Len Goodall, kept the Union Inn on the Wednesfield Road, now demolished like so many other pubs in the town.

Joseph Alan Price, born 1926

Previous page The wedding of Bill and Rose Price in the coalyard owned by the groom's father in Vincent Street.

Left The Warwick Arms on the corner of St Mary's Terrace in the Irish Quarter, off Stafford Street.

Below The entrance to the last blacksmiths' yard in Wolverhampton, between Vincent Street and Dawson Street, with Molineux's floodlights visible behind.

The Union Inn, between the canal bridge and the railway bridges on the Wednesfield Road, and usually known as The Bridge. Now demolished.

Blakenhall

My father ran a nursery in Blakenhall in the 1930s. We lived at The Cottage, no. 1 Haggar Street. Kirby's nursery was well known in the area, especially for the tomatoes Dad grew in his greenhouses. I lived there with my twin brother, Stanley, and my other brother, Cyril, and we used to help in the nursery. It's hard to believe there was a nursery in Blakenhall now; it was all cleared away after the war.

Margaret Fletcher (*née* Kirby)

Tettenhall Wood

I was born in the Royal Oak in Tettenhall Wood because my father, Dan Watkins, had been called up into the Royal Air Force and sent to Cyprus, and my mother, Olive, had to vacate her house, which was let to a family. We lived with my grandparents, Henry James and Elizabeth Darby, who kept the pub, for the six years of the war. Tettenhall Wood was a wonderful place, a little village, with no bus service up the hill.

We had a huge garden and one of the people in the village used to keep pigs there, so we always had bacon, and at another point we had a goat to keep the grass short on the bowling green. I can't remember if we milked the goat, but I can remember the milk lady coming with a cart on which there was a jug and a churn, which was how we had our milk – it didn't come in a bottle.

Eventually we had a donkey, which belonged to a girl called Anne Woodall who lived on the Holloway. I understand the donkey came from Blackpool to Tettenhall

Wood on the bus, whoever was in charge having persuaded them to let him on, and the conductor had the sack for that.

The donkey was called Toby and we used to give walks up the lane at the side of the pub for a penny a ride, if you could get him to move. We had a collecting box for the Church of England's Children's Society and we regularly used to send money off.

Margaret Little's mother was the only person who could get the donkey to move with any success. We used to be in the lane with carrots, pushing and shoving, trying to get the donkey to give us our penny ride, but it didn't always work. The donkey was normally kept on the bowling green at the pub, and of course there was no bowling during the war.

There was also an air-raid shelter at the back of the pub, which was like an open garage upstairs, and underneath there were three rooms, which was the shelter. I can remember a notice which said 'Air-raid shelter for 55 people', which was about the sum total of the population of Tettenhall Wood. The air-raid siren was on the Institute by the crossroads, and when the siren went I can remember going down there. At one point my mother said she had had enough of that, and that she would not go down any more, but she was made to.

I didn't like the school, which was next door where the library is now. I was taken to school and was told I would like it. I had only been there about half an hour and I decided I didn't like it and I came home. I had to be taken back again.

I was at the school until my father came home, and I remember that day vividly. He

Opposite The Rose and Crown in
Tettenhall Wood, two cottages
alongside.

Right Donkey rides in Tettenhall Wood.
On the donkey is Ann Surman and,
behind her, Graham Goodall. To the left
is Anne Goodall and, behind her,
Margaret Little, who lived in the cottages
next to the Royal Oak. The other girl is
Margaret Lewis.

was due to come at four o'clock in the after-noon. You could not buy clothes, but my mother was very handy with a needle and thread, and she made me a yellow and white striped dress for the occasion. He came early, while I was in school, and I saw these two faces over the glass door, my mother and this man, who I had never seen. The teacher said I could go home, but I didn't want to go home then; I had grown to like school. Anyway I did, and I was stood on the dining table and this dress was put on, and I took him down the garden and showed him my straw-berry patch, as I had a little veg garden. That was it really, I wasn't interested after that. I had never seen him, of course, since I was a baby, as he could not get leave, being based in Cyprus. My Grandfather had been my Dad. When we moved back to our house in Fallings Park I was allowed back to the Royal Oak for weekends, so that I got used to the move, and I have to say my father and I became the best of pals.

Anne Surman, born 1940

Perton Ridge

After we got married my husband, John, was working at Goodyear. He hated it. I've been in that place and the smell of rubber was awful. We wanted to get a house of our own. We were living in Coventry Street with my mother, my sister, her husband Jack and their two children. John said he could get a tied cottage if he got a job gardening or something like that, so he wrote to Colonel Hatton, who lived at Westbeech near Pattingham, who was advertising for a gardener. Colonel and Mrs

Hatton came to Coventry Street to see him. He didn't know before then that John came from Kingswood, which was only just down the road from Westbeech, so he got the job, even though four others had already been interviewed.

Colonel Hatton was the Estate Manager for the Wrottesley Park Estate, and John did gardening for him and also worked as a woodman on the estate. We went there in August 1947 and our son, Alec, was born in October. We got one of the Slings Cottages on Perton Ridge. It was old, but it was the best of a block of four, with a long garden. It had a

kitchen attached with running water, and we had a black-lead fireplace. I got a bit fed-up of that after a bit and eventually Colonel Hatton put us a tile grate in. And we'd got three bedrooms. The toilet was all the way down the garden and round the corner. John used to stand by the back door if I wanted to use it at night, I was that scared of the dark.

We were alright there; we were happy there for five years. To start with we only had a primus stove to cook on, and we bought an electric cooker – it was only £16. I don't know what we ate, the rations were so little. We had eggs from Colonel Hatton, and John

Opposite left Leah and John Brew at the time they moved to the Slings Cottage on Perton Ridge.

Opposite right Colonel Christopher Hatton JP, of Westbeech House, Wolverhampton, who had helped form the TA and commanded the 213 Field Company of the Royal Engineers through the First World War.

Right The Star and Garter Hotel, Victoria Street, with Preedy's tobacconists just beyond.

would get pheasants during the shooting season, but I didn't like pheasant. There were plenty of rabbits, and I remember going down the steps which lead down to the bottom of the ridge from the bottom of our garden and seeing dozens of them. John showed me how to set a snare, which he knew how to do, being a country lad, and I set one. I went down to check it next day, and there was a rabbit with his foot in it hopping about trying to get loose. It was awful, I had to wait for John to come home to kill it.

John had Friday off and we used to go with our baby son, Alec, wrapped in a shawl, shopping in Wolverhampton. We used to go in a tobacconist's shop opposite Beatties, just above the Star and Garter in Victoria Street, to buy his cigarettes; he smoked Capstan Full Strength. One day there was an old man in front of us, dressed anyhow in an old coat, who wanted to look at a pipe in the window. While we were waiting the girl got it out of the window, and the man turned it over and over, and I thought 'I wish he'd hurry up', and he asked her how much it was. When she told him he gave it her back and she put it back in the window and he left. I thought it was a shame, poor old man, and I would

The Slings Cottage into which Leah and John Brew moved, but shown in 1916, with Mrs Malin and her daughter outside.

have bought it for him if I'd got enough money. Then John got his cigarettes and, when we went out, he said, 'Do you know who that man was?'

I said, 'No.'

He said, 'He's my boss, Lord Wrottesley.'

I said, 'Good Lord, I nearly bought him that pipe.'

When John told Colonel Hatton about it, he told Lord Wrottesley: 'I told you, you ought to smarten yourself up. My gardener's wife nearly bought you that pipe that you were looking at last Friday.'

Leah Brew, born 1925

two
At School

Alec Brew's coronation picture in 1953, taken at Codsall Primary School.

Codsall School

I started school when I was five, which would be in 1896, I suppose. We were in the room at the far end next to the mill. The woman in there was Mrs Patton; she lived down Sandy Lane on the left-hand side and she learned us the alphabet, parrot fashion, and counting, twice one is two, the tables etc. When we finished with her we went on to the next little room, where the seats inclined up, with a woman named Mrs Phillips; she lived right opposite the church. She was another motherly woman; she carried on with our tables but she also learned us to write. The first thing she learned us was to write our names and address. Of course there was no writing paper and pencils, there was slates and pencils, and the Bible and the prayer book. We played in the far playground with the girls.

When we finished with Mrs Phillips we came into the big room. The partitions were put in there while I was at the school. Here my first teacher was Mrs Wilkes, if I remember right, and I was a year with her, and then I went into the next class with Mrs Cockerill, Miss Jones as she was then, as she was engaged to be married.

We had to fall into our classes outside when the bell started ringing, at about ten minutes to nine, and if you were in the square when that started ringing, you had to make haste to get up there. If you were late and they had gone in, well you just had to go inside the door and to stand there and wait until Mr Plant decided to look up and see you there. If you'd got a reasonable excuse you got away with it, but if you didn't have a good excuse the cane came off the hook at the side of his desk. He used to catch hold of the cane with his gloved right hand; they reckoned it was a cork hand, I don't know whether he'd had an accident or something. You had to stick your hand out and down would come the cane, and mind if it didn't tingle, and he'd send you to the back of the class. The walls were painted, so that when you got to the back you'd put your hand on it to take the sting out.

The girls and boys came from the one side of Kingswood Common, from the Bradshaws and from Wrottesley Lodge. The dividing line was County Lane, those on one side went to Codsall School, those on the other to Albrighton. Dam Mill, Oaken Lawn, Bilbrook, they all had to walk a three-mile radius. There were no tarred roads then and no street lighting. You had to have a good pair of shoes, and the roads were muddy in winter.

I finished school when I was thirteen, I was tall for my age, I think I was as tall as I am now, and of course I was anxious to get to

Mrs Barley with her infants class in 1919, in the classroom where Dan Brew was first taught.

Edith Baron, on the left, playing tennis with the upper-sixth at Wolverhampton Girls' High in the 1920s.

work. I thought someone else would do it all, but I needn't have worried.

Dan Brew, born 1891

Wolverhampton Girls' High School

My mother, Alice, died nine months after I was born and I was brought up by my aunt and uncle on Young Willie Buck's farm, at Rowley near Pattingham. I went to Wolverhampton Girls' High School, which had been founded jointly by Wolverhampton and Staffordshire Councils in the year I was born. It took ninety girls from each council, and I was one of the Staffordshire girls, of course. From 1927, the number of Staffordshire girls was reduced to one third of the intake.

Edith Baron, born 1911

St Michael's School, Tettenhall

We lived in Nursery Walk, Tettenhall. I went to Tettenhall School until I was nearly eight. I started school with my cousin Ronnie, who lived two doors away, and was the same age. We came home at playtime, thinking it was home time. I can see mother now, she was there cleaning the steel fender to the fire. She had to take her apron off, wash her hands and take us back to school. I had a mother who never got cross, a lovely mother. She was only fifty-one when she died – very sad.

My teacher was Mrs Perry. They had a fish shop in Whitmore Reans, and she used to teach sewing and that sort of thing. Then there was Miss Morton from Codsall, a big woman she was; she used to come on an upright bike. She was the cookery and laundry teacher, because we had cookery Wednesday and laundry on Thursday. Mr Westerman taught the boys for woodwork. Then the other teachers were Miss Lockley,

who lived in Regis Road with her brother and sister. He was a bachelor and they were spinsters. I don't know what her brother did but Miss Lockley's sister was a demonstrator for the Gas Offices. Another teacher was Miss Till. The Tills kept the Shoulder of Mutton in Wood Road. Then there was Mr Pickard and Mr Rex, who taught in the modern way.

I don't regret my school days at all, I loved being at school.

Betty Kyte, born 1919

Kingswood School

I went to school when I was five. Kingswood School had one classroom, and we were there until we were eight. The common was more open then, a few people kept goats and fowl on it when the little school up the common was in use. When you came out of school, it was all grass, no trees. There was a lot of gorse, not much bracken.

Mrs Shaw gave a very good grounding. She was a very patient woman. She had a useless hulk of a husband who never did a day's work in his life: he suffered with his nerves. She taught simple arithmetic, how to write and spell. It was a Church school, and I suppose from the same age I attended Sunday school. One's reward for attendance was going on the yearly outing. The first one I can recall we went to the Clent Hills in charabancs, open-topped, and driving one of them was Don Everall himself. We went to places like Rhyl and Aberystwyth. I went to Sunday school till I was about fourteen. I never joined the choir though.

The school was the centre of the village's life. Almost weekly in the winter were things like whist drives, and a dance once a week. Half the night there'd be whist and then a two- or three-piece band came in, or even a piano, and we danced. Other weeks there'd be

Kingswood children and parents just outside the wall of the school, on the common in the 1920s.

Kingswood children and parents outside their school on Kingswood Common

what they called a social, which was more or less a dance with a few daft games thrown in – everyone used to go. Now it's no longer a community, the school's a private house of course. There's no community, there's just a collection of houses, though there are more of them.

We were mischievous but never destructive. There were certain things that were permissible if you could get away with them, like scrumping fruit, or fishing where you shouldn't, or a bit of poaching. We all collected eggs. Those sort of things were against established society, because you accepted that if you got caught you got a good hiding on the spot. It

was no good going home to my Dad saying someone's hit me, because you were likely to get a further one for being a blasted nuisance. It was the same with the local policeman; if he caught you up to mischief you got a good hiding on the spot, no magistrates' court. It certainly taught you to be more careful.

John Brew, born 1922

All Saints School

I went to All Saints School in 1925. There were two infant teachers both called Brown, Big Miss Brown and Little Miss Brown. The head was Mr Boon and he was known as

Daddy Boon. Boys I remember include Billy Lowe, from Maxwell Street, who was a good footballer, and Horace Quillam of Gordon Street who played for the Town Boys, as did Horace Mattox of Dartmouth Street. Alec Gilroy went to the grammar school and was a Sunday school teacher. He was ordained and served as a curate at St Thomas, Wednesfield, before becoming a canon at Portsmouth or Southampton. Leonard Roberts also went to the grammar school and got a scholarship to university, I think. He won an MC in 1943 with the 43rd Division.

Of the girls I remember Lily Grafton from Steelhouse Lane, who later had a paper shop, and Joan Harriman of All Saints Road, who was the niece of Miss Reynolds, an infant teacher; she later went to the Girls High School.

I remember that if we boys left school in time we could help drive cattle through the town. Teddy Turner, known as 'the cow walloper', was employed by Nock & Joseland to move cattle from the cattle auction on Bilston Road to their destination.

Ken Goodman, born 1920

Albrighton School

At eight I went to school at Albrighton, in Station Road, which seemed like a huge place to me. I think I was lucky there because the headmaster, Mr Smith, known as Dickie Smith behind his back, his priority was to teach you things he thought would be of benefit. He was in a small village in a rural community; he wasn't going to breed a race of academics. Arithmetic was of the highest standard, we got a good hand at English, and a greater emphasis on general knowledge, modern rather than history. He pointed out what was going to happen in Germany almost

All the children of Albrighton School in the 1920s. Headmaster 'Dickie' Smith is in the centre and John Brew is second from the right in the back row.

Above Three Air Training Corps (ATC) cadets. Left to right: Keith Campbell, Fred Wright and Les Broadfield.

Left Les Broadfield and his sister Marie in the garden of their house in Springfield.

in perfect detail. I was there in 1933 when Hitler came to power.

John James Brew, born 1920

St Stephen's School

I went to St Stephen's School just by Butler's Brewery. I remember the layout of the school, there was a big partition across the main hall. I remember Miss Hassell, who was the daughter of the vicar of St Stephen's, and I remember being in the hall with my little brother one day and for some reason, I don't know what it was, Miss Hassell showed me a penny and a

halfpenny and she said: 'Which are you going to have?' and of course I had the penny and my little brother Tony had the halfpenny. It was probably something we had done, some errand, or for the work we'd done.

I remember at lunchtime, when we went out to play, there would be all the mothers round the railings with bread and jam, and all the children would go round the railings to get their big pieces of bread and jam, or a bit of cake or something. None of them had to come very far. I lived just down Beacon Street at no. 25, only 100 yards away. Beacon Street isn't there any more.

When I was nine we had a tragedy in the family and my mother didn't want to live there any more, so we moved to Low Hill and I went to Bushbury Hill School.

I joined the ATC (Air Training Corps) when I was sixteen. I was in 1047 Squadron, B Flight, Bushbury Hill, based at the school. Later we went to Clarkson's in Snow Hill to do drill. At the back there was part of an aeroplane, just a fuselage, we never used it though. Fred Wright became the Flight Sergeant and I became Sergeant.

Les Broadfield, born 1925

Willenhall Road Schools

When I was eleven years of age I passed my school exams, which gained me a place at Wolverhampton's Girls' High School, but my parents, not being rich people, could not afford to let me go there. I was lucky that I had a caring mother and a hardworking father. I attended Willenhall Road School which included a senior girls' high school.

My favourite lesson was domestic science. The school had a small flat, and two girls would spend a fortnight in it, doing no lessons at all. They would cook teachers' lunches, planning the meals themselves, shopping for the food. We had to light a fire each morning, make the bed, although no one had slept in it, clean the windows and do the washing. I found this training very valuable to me in future years. I loved it all and I had made up my mind when I left school that I wanted to be a cook in a large establishment.

Leah Brew, born 1925

Eastfield Secondary Modern School

I went to Moseley Village School and then went to Eastfield Secondary Modern, as it had just become. It used to be Willenhall Road School. I passed the eleven-plus and went for an interview at Bilston Girls' High School with another girl. The other girl went there, but I had a thing about all my mother's relatives who were buried in the cemetery right next to Bilston Girls' High and I didn't want to go, I don't know why. I went to Eastfield instead.

There was a flat at the side of the cookery room and the girls all had a stint in the flat, looking after it, two at a time, and cooking meals for the teachers. I don't think they would have enjoyed my cooking; I was more sporty and I used to like to get on the hockey field. We also had to have a week in the nursery, looking after the little ones, practice being a mother.

I was one of the first people who had to stop on until they were fifteen. They hadn't got a clue what to do with people for that extra year. It was a complete waste of time.

Florence Quinton (*née* Roberts), born 1934

All Saints and St Peter's Schools

The highlight of the year at All Saints was May Day. There was a May Queen chosen, maypole dancing etc. Goodness knows how mothers managed during the war years, but all the boys had new grey short flannels and white shirts, and the girls new white dresses – my auntie was a dressmaker in Tettenhall Wood and made mine. All the children got new white socks and crepe-soled brown sandals, and everyone took part. I remember flowers everywhere.

Mr Lancaster, who lodged in Vicarage Road, loved dancing, He formed the morris dancers and the girls' country dancing team. The groups competed at Leamington Spa and Cheltenham every year, often winning.

A crocodile of children progressed from All Saints to Monmore Green School every day for school dinners. All Saints had no facilities of its own.

Children that were confirmed at All Saints Church and continued attending church went to St Peter's at eleven years old. I was lucky enough to attend this wonderful school, which was by the wholesale market. The boys occupied the upstairs and the girls the downstairs. They had a headmaster, we a most wonderful headmistress, Miss Postlewaite. Boys and girls never intermingled, except in the tuck shop in North Road. The trees in the boys' playground are still there as part of the university.

Mercy Jackson, born 1938

three

At Play

Detail of the Compton football team on the playground at Tettenhall Wood School in the early 1950s.

The Territorial Army

When the Territorial Army was formed in the middle of 1908, I was between sixteen and seventeen and the big attraction was the holiday with pay by the seaside. Of course you normally daren't have asked for a holiday, as you had no money to go on holiday as things were. The first holiday was at Towyn, North Wales; lovely sunny weather, and we had a shilling a day, and that was a lot of pocket money then. We went to Towyn twice in 1908 and 1909, the third place was in Derbyshire, near Buxton, three miles out at a place called Hindlow, and the fourth and last in 1911 was at Abergavenny, during a very hot and dry summer; the grass verges were dried out and there were no tarred roads, and when there was a motor car the dust used to go up in white clouds so that the hedges were white. We were on the side of the mountain and the water was rationed.

We were the 6th South Staffords, based in Wolverhampton. The HQ was a very big drill hall in Stafford Street, the whole battalion could parade in there. There was a rifle range in Sedgley behind the Fighting Cocks. It went back 600 yards, but with the machine gun we had to get in close, because of the danger of spraying bullets up into Sedgley. We fired there a time or two.

The most important thing that happened when I was in the Terriers was the Coronation of King George V, and I was one of a detachment of twenty-five who went to London for that. I think we got a shilling a day, but we had to buy some special shoes, and that did away with that. They said, 'the Honour'. You can believe me there was some blinking honour attached to that. We were drilling for weeks, presenting arms and standing at ease, fixing bayonets.

We were camped in Kensington Gardens, ten men to a bell tent. We were in red tunics, white belts, buttoned up to the eyeholes. We were in position at five in the morning, in Pall Mall, just to the left of the Haymarket. We were eight deep and all of the roads were packed with people who had been there all night. We had one bottle of water between five of us and three hard biscuits, as big as the top of a cup, and as hard as a cup!

I was in the rear rank between these horses. The horses had been standing a long while, and I suppose they were restless. Then we had orders to fix bayonets and this one horse got more restless. The procession had started to move, and just as the Coronation Coach got level with us, up went this blinking horse on its hind legs. The trooper came out of the saddle and into the road. There was me trying

The Territorial Camp at Hindlow, Derbyshire, in 1911.

Soldiers of the Territorial Army in 1908, at camp in Towyn. Dan Brew is fifth from the left on the back row.

to hold this rifle and bayonet, with a point as sharp as a needle, holding that and trying not to hurt him, and there was this struggling horse and the trooper on the ground. I just managed to look sideways as the coach went by, and the king and queen looked bored to death, and they looked sideways and saw this job as was going on with us. Somebody snatched the trooper out of the way and the horse went on his hind legs again.

We had to stand there an hour after the procession had gone by. We had been there all day from five in the morning to five at night, with nothing but the water and the biscuits. When we got back to Kensington Gardens they said we'd have a wonderful meal of stew. Believe me there was nothing cooked, and as for going into town to get something that was hopeless, you had to make the best of it.

The latrines were a big trench, no seats, with a piece of sacking in front. You could imagine what that place was like, 200-300 blokes there. And what amused me was there

was this couple walking through Kensington Gardens and she was curious as what was going on behind the sacking, and she went over and looked over the top, but she went away a damn sight quicker!

The folks at home had had a wonderful time, and they said what a wonderful thing it was. Well, it was a wonderful thing, twelve blinking hours standing in the street, bottle of water between five of us and three hard biscuits. How anyone did for a run out, I don't know, there was nowhere to ease yourself. We packed up the second day and came back to civilisation.

Dan Brew, born 1892

Floral Fête and flying

Before the First World War, the principal outdoor event in Wolverhampton was the annual Floral Fête. It was three days in July, the event culminating each day in a grand firework display masterminded by the well-known fireworks firm of Brocks of Crystal Palace.

The hangars erected for the first all-British Flying Meeting at Dunstall Park in June 1910. The first three are for Claude Grahame White (Farman biplane), Cecil Grace, (Shorts biplane), George Cockburn (Farman biplane and H.J.D. Astley (Lane monoplane).

The Hartill monoplane at Dunstall Park, built by a Wolverhampton plumber. It was one of the aircraft which did not manage to leave the ground.

The Seddon 'Mayfly' at Dunstall Park in 1919. Called 'the bicycle plane' because it was built by Accles & Pollock of Oldbury, who also made tubing for bikes, it was the largest aeroplane in the world at the time, but never flew. The Mann & Overton monoplane in the background gives scale.

Regarding aviation, the first event I recall was an air balloon ascent from near the railway arches at Dunstall Park, and a spectacular event of a parachute descent from a balloon by a lady parachutist, Dolly Shepherd. In 1910–11 a lot of my time was spent in the vicinity of Dunstall Park watching amateur and professional aviators attempting to get their planes off the ground. At that time the enthusiastic aeronauts were glad of the help of even boys to push their aeroplanes out of the hangars. There were seven hangars backing on to the canal from near the railway arches, six adjoining in a row and another, 100 yards along, backing on to a canal lock. Each hangar contained an aeroplane either complete or being erected. The seventh contained the world-famous 'bicycle plane' which never managed to get off the ground. [The Seddon 'Mayfly' made by Accles & Pollock in Oldbury – A.B.]

The Star monoplane was tested at Dunstall Park. To my inexperienced eye it looked much too heavy for its engine capacity to take off. It never took off, even after many runs over a period of weeks.

On 27 June 1910, there was an aviation meeting at Dunstall Park which drew some of the world-famous names in aviation, including Claude Graham-White with his biplane. I can see him now sitting in front of the pusher propeller, with no protection from the elements, such as a cockpit, cap turned back to front, and wearing a pair of goggles.

Later I saw the famous aviator Gustav Hamel, the first British man to 'loop the loop', giving demonstrations of his prowess in his Bleriot monoplane. He disappeared over the Channel while flying to France in 1914.

On 4, 5 and 6 August 1918, there was a great charity event at Dunstall Park composed largely of circus acts. One of them was a sixty foot high wire by a Monsieur Ponchery who wheeled a wheelbarrow across the wire with his two sons in the wheelbarrow. I have good reason to remember this because Mr Ponchery and his family then lived in Bushbury, whilst his two sons were schoolmates of mine at Bushbury Lane (New) School, opened in January 1910, now called Oxley Primary School.

Cyril Jones, born 1900

The Palais

We used to go to the Hippodrome for a Saturday night out, or the Palais in Temple Street, what's called The Beach now. We used

QUEENS SQUARE, WOLVERHAMPTON. 2426

The Hippodrome at the bottom of Queen Square, with Charlie Kunz, Arthur Prince and Les Allen on the bill.

to go dancing there. Percy used to go on a Saturday afternoon to learn, and then he taught me on a Saturday night. That's how we learned to dance.

Betty Kyte, born 1919

The Hippodrome

I like looking back to my visits to the old Hippodrome, opposite Beatties, where Yates Wine Lodge is now situated, and where I was privileged to see stars such as Joseph Locke, Old Mother Riley, Dick Tracy (The Street Singer), Kevin O'Connor etc. Very enjoyable memories. In 1956 I qualified with the St John's Ambulance and attended my first official function at the Odeon, Dunstall. Later I was to attend as the regular first aid man at the Penn Cinema. The film *The Angry Silence* was first premiered there with a midnight screening, with Sir Richard Attenborough in attendance with several other stars. A gentleman called Gordon Minton was the manager.

Arthur Maker

Playing with Stan Cullis

I played at the Molineux for Bushbury Lane School in the Town Under-Eleven Cup. We beat Prestwood Road School 3-1, and I was centre forward and scored two goals. There were two Joneses, two Turners and two Evanses in the team, none of them related. Bill Lowton, who was the Wolves captain, was watching. In the dressing room there was a deep bath, about ten foot square, and Billy Lowton chucked us in. He brought us a cup of tea at half time as well. Arthur Turner was one of the team, and he played for Grimsby Town later on. Billy Harrison was scout for Grimsby. He used to play for Wolves, and he also played bowls – he was a bowls fanatic. He

wanted me to go with Arthur, but I was interested in electrics and I wanted to stay at ECC.

I played with Stan Cullis later on. I played for the Wolverhampton Gas Company, who had a pitch behind the works, and the Wolves 'leftovers', those who didn't play for the first team, the reserves or the youth team, played in this team with mostly gas company players. Major Buckley used to come and watch us. I played inside left and Stan Cullis played left half.

Harry Jones, born 1917

Stafford Pageant

Every year Butler's Brewery used to send a float to the Stafford Pageant. It was mostly done by the forwarding department, the drivers, including my father. They took on a theme, it might be something from Dickens, or a particular pub, or Robin Hood. I remember going to Stafford, it would be in the mid-1930s, and we would wait by the side of the road, and there would be different floats from different factories, and we would wait for the Butler's float to come by and gave a big cheer when I saw my Dad. Then they used to go back to the brewery and have a big booze-up.

Les Broadfield, born 1925

Park Village

I used to come home from work at Henry Meadows of an evening, have my tea, and then I had a mate who lived two doors away, his parents kept a chip shop, and we used to be off round the pubs mainly. We used to go on various runs; we always used to meet in the Park Inn and then we would decide where we were going. We would go up Park Lane to the Paget Arms and have a drink in the Paget, and then get the bus up to Showell Circus and the pubs up there. The other route was up to

Butler's float for one of the Stafford pageants in the 1930s, with a Robin Hood theme. It is in the yard at the Springfield Brewery. Aylie Broadfield is third from the left in the front row.

Wednesfield to the Prestwood Arms, the Pear Tree and the pubs round there, and then the third route was up to town. Opposite the Park Inn was a bus stop; and it was on the bus and straight up to Stafford Street, and then we'd go to the Greyhound or the Vine Hotel, what'd be the Hogshead now, and one or two others. Then we'd walk home and stop at a chip shop on the way, for threepenny worth of chips. Sometimes we stopped at two chip shops if we was hungry. The funny thing was that my mate lived in a chip shop but we used to pay for our chips.

I always used to remember the Efandem wenches coming out of work. Their faces and hands were black, covered in carbon from the batteries. A lot of them lived in Featherstone, so they used to walk to the Cannock Road to catch their bus, and they used to drop in the chip shop for their fish and chips, still covered in black, and as they ate their chips their fingers would slowly turn white, as the carbon rubbed off on the chips.

George Brazier, born 1927

The 1939 Cup Final

I used to have some pretty footwork, dancing, because I used to play outside right for the local team, Compton, and as a winger you have to be light on your feet. We played in the sand hollow at Compton where the Working Men's Club was built later, but we also had other pitches. We used the pitch in the Dutch Camp in Wrottesley Park, and a field at Danescourt, and at Claregate Playing Fields.

Above Wolves' supporters at Low Level Station in 1939, off to watch the Cup Final. They were less happy on their return.

Below Compton FC outside the door of the Claregate pub, with Percy Kyte second from the left in the front row.

The Compton football team on the playground at Tettenhall Wood School in the early 1950s.

When we played there we got changed in the Claregate pub.

I went to the Cup Final in 1939, when the Wolves were expected to win about 10-1 and they lost 4-1. I had to work a double shift at Goodyear to go, and on the way back on the train I was dead tired and I fell asleep, and the others shoved a sausage in my flies and waited for people's reaction, wondering what it was.

Betty was so mad about me going to the match she went dancing at the Palais without me, with a friend. I was mad about that. She got a lift home to Compton in a car as well.

I went to the other Cup Finals in 1949 and 1960 as well, and we won those, so I saw two wins and a loss, so that wasn't too bad, but we should have beaten Portsmouth in 1939.

Percy Kyte, born 1916

The 1949 Cup Final

I missed the 1949 Cup Final against Leicester. I'd seen all the games in the early rounds, and I had got my Final ticket, and I couldn't go on the day of the Final, I'd got the flu. I sold my rail ticket and my Final ticket to a fellow who lived in the same village, Ettingshall. It was terrible, my mother wouldn't let me go, I was only about thirteen. I was ill though, when I stood up my head was spinning round.

Geoff Bates, born 1934

Dancing at the Civic

I had been ill in the RAF and got a posting down to Cosford. I teamed up with a friend of mine, named Bill Price, and we would go dancing at the Civic, which had big bands, every Thursday and Saturday night. Saturday afternoon we used to go to the pictures and then from the pictures we used to go to Market Street. There used to be a nice cafe there, we'd have a meal and then go to the Civic.

One night we were in the bar and we were with two girls. That bar used to be jam-packed, and that night Bill wanted to go up

to the balcony to sit down. The girls would-
n't come up, so we went up there for a rest
and a smoke, and when we came down we
started looking for some new women. We
always used to stand by the band on the stage,
and I spotted this girl in the far corner, and I
thought, 'She looks alright, I'll make a go for
her'; that was my wife Flo. I lived in Codsall,
she lived in Coventry Street off the Willenhall
Road, so we just used to meet up at the Civic.

Sometimes we used to ring Denis Housden
in Codsall, who kept Housden's Stores but
also ran a taxi. So he used to come and pick
us up and we would run Flo home. It was
always hectic getting on the last bus. The
dances finished at eleven o'clock and the last
bus went just after that. One night the last bus
to Codsall was packed, everybody standing,
and we got on it, but the conductor rang the
bell and stopped the bus, and said we had to
get off. When we got off, another bloke
jumped on, so we ran after it and jumped back
on again. The conductor rang the bell again
and stopped the bus.

'I've told you two,' he said, 'you'll have to
get off.'

'He's just got on,' I said, 'If we're getting off
he's getting off.'

'I can't turn him off,' he said, 'He's an
inspector!'

We wouldn't get off until this bloke get off,
and there was a long argument, and in the end
we asked the bloke to show us his identifica-
tion, to prove he was an inspector, and he
hadn't got any, so he had to get off. So did we;
we had to get a taxi back.

Harry Law, born 1925

Wolves and West Brom

I used to play football for Heath Town Wesley,
the Wesleyan Chapel team; in fact I was the
captain. We were all friends together, all

Billy Wright with the League Championship trophy in
1954, the first time Wolves had won it.

muckers, always stuck together. Johnny
Nicholls was one of the team, and one day he
said, 'I've been signed on by the Baggies'. He
played in the A Team, the reserves and so
forth, until he got in the first team. He played
with Ronnie Allen, and they called it Ronnie
for Johnny, because Ronnie used to put the
passes through and he scored; he scored
thirty-two goals in one season. He played with
Ronnie Allen in the England team at
Hampden Park against Scotland, when
England won 4-2, and Ronnie and Johnny
got a goal each.

I used to go with him to watch the Baggies.
You know the way they drive up to matches
in their Mercedes these days, well me and

Above Billy Wright with seventy-one of his international caps and all his medals and awards. He eventually won 105 caps.

Right The unused ticket for the Wolves match against Honved in 1954, their first under floodlights.

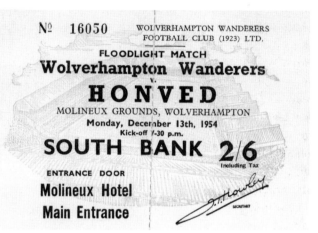

Johnny used to go on the bus, and we used to have to change at Wednesbury. He got £10 a week to play for the first team, and I think it was £2 bonus for a win and £1 for a draw. I was getting £8 at Bayliss, Jones & Bayliss. Both me and Johnny were Wolves' fans actually, but I used to watch him play for the Albion.

In 1954 he played for them when they won the Cup, and they were runners-up to the Wolves in the League. They lost to Wolves twice, 1-0, and Wolves won the League by 4 points. So they came close to doing the Double, the first team to do it for ages. In 1947, in the first season after the war, the last match of the season was against Liverpool, and Wolves would have won the League for the first time if they had won that match, in fact they only had to draw to win the League on goal average. Wolves had three international goalkeepers on their books, Bert Williams, Cyril Sidlow for Wales and Noel Dwyer, the Irishman. At the beginning of the season they transferred Sidlow to Liverpool, and they were drawing one each, and Wolves were all over Liverpool, and Cyril Sidlow was pulling off saves all over the place. They had a centre forward called Albert Stubbings, and him and Stan Cullis were on the halfway line. Sidlow kicked the ball right up into the Wolves half and there was Cullis, about a yard behind Stubbings, all the way to the penalty area, and he scored the winner. Cullis could have tripped him up and Wolves would have won the League. That was Stan's last match.

We had to wait until 1954 to win the League, when Billy Wright was captain. He was a great player. His distribution, and the way he tackled, it wasn't man or ball, it was always the ball with Billy.

I remember the Honved match against Wolves, also in 1954, Puskas and all that. England had just lost their first match at Wembley, 6–3 to Hungary, and many of the team, including Puskas, were in the Honved team which Wolves arranged to play under their new floodlights. It was 2s 6d to get in and I left a ticket for a friend of mine for the match at the turnstiles as I knew the guy on the turnstile. However he had to work and he couldn't come. Honved were winning 2–0 at half time and we thought it was just a matter of how many goals, but they came out in the second half and you've never seen anything like it. Wolves won 3–2 and Roy Swinburne scored two goals near the end. The crowd was huge, and they swayed up and down the terraces. If you'd got your hands in your pockets you couldn't get them out. It was a marvellous game.

Doug Quinton, born 1930

Allotments

I have had an allotment ever since I came to Blakeley Avenue in 1957. The allotments were a picture then. I used to collect the rents

Stan Seiboth addressing the Royal Air Force Association dinner in 1987.

and I had a waiting list. They were built after the war on what was just waste ground. They have gone to rack and ruin now. They were beautiful. We could look out from our bedroom and it was all cultivated. There was an old railway chap who used to grow the most beautiful sweet peas, and further up a man who had great big chrysanthemums, and they just grew them for enjoyment. Of course this was out in the country then. Since the Dovecotes Estate was built across the railway, people started to walking across the railway and through the allotments for a shortcut.

Stan Seiboth, born 1924

four

At Work

Dan Brew on his first ganger's trolley on the Tettenhall Line in the 1920s.

As Mayor

I was first asked to stand as a councillor in 1965. I had been in the Conservatives for years, and the year I was selected I never thought I would get on, because I was up against a very strong candidate. It was in Oxley Ward, the boundaries have changed since. It was very much more gentlemanly in those days, and of course you never got paid, you never even received expenses. You even had to buy a cup of tea, and you had to pay for the telephone. It was more sort of a voluntary thing, without the political angle that you have today. It was for the good of the town.

The year I was mayor, in 1987, was one of the highlights of my thirty-five years on the council. Bishan Dass, the mayor, was one of six Labour councillors who had lost their seats. The flowerboxes in Queen Square, that had done it. When we were canvassing, it didn't matter if the rates had gone up a hundredfold, there were no queries about the rates. It was all about those flowerboxes, and six Labour councillors lost their seats because of them, and Dass, the mayor, was one of them. Of course until the vote for the new mayor is actually taken, Dass still had a vote, and it was the casting vote. There were thirty Labour councillors on the left and thirty Conservatives and Liberal Democrats on the right, and he had the casting vote.

I went into the mayor-making that evening, and beforehand someone had telephoned me and said, 'I think there's going to be fun and games tonight, and you could well be mayor'. I said, 'Oh, come off it,' just like that, 'Come off it'.

Stan, my husband, wasn't going to come with me. He said he had seen enough of these votes and he wasn't going to come, but I said if I was going to lose by just one vote, I should want him there, so he came. When it came to the vote there was one Labour councillor in hospital, so Dass did not get to use his casting vote, because we were one over. It was all still, and when it suddenly dawned on people, our side absolutely erupted. You couldn't hear yourself think.

The clerk came to me and asked me to come with him, and on the back of a piece of paper I had just put a few hurried words, and I was very glad I did. I said that in my case there had been no rehearsal as it said on the programme, I did not know the agenda, to take charge of the meeting or anything. My sister, Mary Machin, was going to be my consort, and she was sitting right at the back. And she asked one of the officials if she could go forward and he said, 'I'm afraid you can't,

Madame,' and she said, 'I think I can, because I'm the mayor's sister'.

I had just got the robe and was sitting there next to the Chief Executive, and Mary comes up, ever so nervous, and she has her badge put on. I got up and said, 'Mary, you'll be alright, love, don't worry'. I was supposed to be sitting there, you know, in state, and I can always remember Mike Lyons telling me to stay where I was, but I ignored him; everything was very relaxed. When we went into the meal afterwards, we had said beforehand that we would

Left Doreen Seiboth, Mayor of Wolverhampton, with her sister, Mary Machin, on the phone to Liliam Webb, Mayor in Georgia, USA, on the launch of a new BT service.

Below Doreen Seiboth with a delegation from the Shanghai Bicycle Company to Daniel Smith Ltd, in the mayor's parlour at the Civic Centre in 1987.

not be going, because I hadn't for a number of years. We hadn't got a seat. Everything was so hurried. My name, 'Councillor Mrs Seiboth, Mayor of Wolverhampton', was written on the back of an envelope. Phil Richards thought he was going to be mayor and he was all decked up ready, but that was that. People said they had never seen anything like it, and I don't think they will again, you know.

The funny thing was we had told Mary's husband, Mo, we would bring him some fish and chips home, from the Avion Centre. He was sitting there waiting for his fish and chips while all this was going on. And Bernard, the mayor's chauffeur, came to me and said, 'When you're ready,' and I said, 'Ready for what?' and he said, 'The mayoral car.' But I told him I had come with Stan and I was going home with Stan, and he said he had never known that before. The new mayor usually dived straight into the mayoral car. It was all good fun.

We saw the queen when she came to St Peter's Church Millennium, and I was deputy mayor. I had been sworn to absolute secrecy, because I was on the committee which knew she was going to be invited, and apparently if these things leak out the chances of her coming are lessened.

The councillors and their partners were going to be entertained at the Molineux football ground, but they said if I was in the party to welcome her at the church, as I was entitled to as a member of the Millennium Committee, we would miss lunch. I said I would rather have the chance to shake her hand, which I did.

When Princess Diana visited the town in 1997 to open the new central police station, amongst other things, I was lucky enough to be the acting mayor at the time, and was presented to her. She drew huge crowds everywhere she went.

Doreen Seiboth, born 1923

Princess Diana visiting Wolverhampton to open the new Bilston Road Police Station in 1997. Councillor Doreen Seiboth, who was acting mayor at the time, is to the left.

Oxley Sidings

When I first went to work in Oxley Sidings before the First World War, I saw one of the worst sights I ever saw, worse than anything I saw during the war. Three chaps had been caught pinching in the Sidings and had been sacked with a minute's notice, so there were three vacancies. Me and George Meredith from Oaken Lawn and Charlie Jones from Seisdon got the jobs, and we went to live in lodgings in South Street just by the Sidings.

We were in the Yard Gang, doing the two sides, while the Main Line Gang did the main line through the middle, the loops and along the line to Birches. It was a hell of a place, with shunting engines going back and forth. You had to be very careful where you stepped.

After a few weeks we got to know some of the people, like the foremen examiners and some of the wheel-tappers.

One day in June 1910, as we were working we saw one of the younger examiners go by and he had a young lad with him. We found out later that the young lad's mother was a widow, and this was his first job out of school, learning to be an examiner. He was with the young examiner as a greaser, which was the first step, starting as a greaser and oiler, and then becoming a wheel-tapper, and then inspecting loads until you passed the exams.

Apparently they were going to do a job replacing a buffer-casting on a truck. They had detonators with them, and they informed the foreman shunter what they were doing. Of course the foreman shunter's head was full of all the names of the trucks that had to be put on all the trains on all the different roads, so he could not be relied on to remember that someone was working on a truck twenty yards away.

All of a sudden all the brake whistles on all the trains were blowing full blast, and everything came to a standstill. All the men on the downside ran to the upside, climbing the iron ladder to the upper level. We knew something was wrong of course, but being fresh to the job we stayed where we were.

Presently the foreman examiner came by, a man named Charlie, who always wore a hard hat. Then the ganger, Edgington, and the wheel foreman came to see us, and told us what had happened. 'You saw those two men go past you down here?' asked Edgington, 'Well, they're smashed to smithereens. Come on, you three, you'll have to help clear it up.'

Of course we were three country lads and we'd never seen anything like it. Although the lad should have been assigned to keep a look-out, he had been straddling the rail, holding the spanner on, as the nuts were running. The examiner too had been straddling the rail, with the buffer against his chest. Neither had heard the train closing up until it was too late and it had hit them. I never saw a worse sight.

We got two stretchers and put the remains on them. A lot of people from Jones Road and South Street were railway people, and it was surprising how the word got around. We had to carry them to a mortuary in Bushbury, and the road was crowded with people. After we got back from the mortuary they allowed us to have a pint of beer at their expense, and by the time that we got back it was dinnertime. The others were upset and didn't want their dinner, but it didn't upset me that much. I collared my dinner and went to the old engine sheds and watched one or two races (at Dunstall Park Racecourse) until it was time to go to work again. But first thing next morning the ganger must have sussed me out. He said, 'You take a shovel and bury those remains in the sidings.

I've seen dead men all over the place, but that was the most horrible sight I've ever seen, I've never seen anyone as mutilated as those two chaps. The widowed mother was relying on her son, and the other was a new examiner, but he forgot the safety rules.

Dan Brew, born 1892

Beatties

I worked in a shop in Wulfruna House, in Prince's Square. It used to be next to Lazenby's, the travel people, opposite the Royal London Buildings. We sold ladies dresses, underwear and hosiery. Every Wednesday the drovers used to drive the cows from the trains, down Lower Stafford Street, to the cattle market, which was somewhere round Cleveland Road. One day the cows came when I was alone in the shop; they were wandering about and I thought they look a bit

James Beattie's Staff Dance at the Victoria Hotel in the 1930s.

vicious. I was a bit scared, as I was only about seventeen then. One turned round and he made for the shop. We had a long glass door which you just pushed open, and in he came, but I had the presence of mind, as there was no way out the back, to go down the cellar. I did have a shock, and I could hear him crashing into the glass cases, a bull in a dress shop. He got through into the little back room where we had got a display of millinery, hats and things, and he just got in there and tossed all the hats about, you know. He came out of there, and there used to be Rawlings, the barbers, in Lichfield Street, opposite the GPO, and the men were being shaved. He went down the steps there and they had to lasso him with a rope and cart him off. It was quite an exciting day.

I left that shop when I was nineteen and I got a job at Beatties. I worked there in various departments until I got married when I was twenty-seven. I met my husband, Arthur, in Queen Square. He was an electrical engineer at the ECC. We used to meet at Reynolds Restaurant in Queen Square, and in the Oak Room, which was a cafe downstairs at the Queens Cinema. That was the best cinema in Wolverhampton, lovely and white, with a balcony. You could see it from right at the bottom of Darlington Street by St Mark's Church.

Beatties was a lovely place, I was very, very happy there. My boss was a director, Mr Farben senior, one of the directors. There was an annual ball at the Victoria Hotel as it used to be. It was great, though some didn't dance and they wouldn't bother to go.

When I first went to work there I had to be prepared to start in the basement at Christmas. I had tried and tried, it was very difficult to get a job there. They said, 'If you'd like to come there's a job going with the Christmas stuff for children.' While I was there they started to open a sports department in the basement. One of the bosses said he thought they should have a few things to bring the children in with their mothers, to spend money. They had tanks of fish, and a parrot, and a few birds in cages. And they asked would I mind helping to feed them and look after them. And I said I'd do anything, but I'm not cleaning fish out the tanks, thank you very much.

Then I got up on to the ground floor, where you walk in, and that's where I was happiest, because I was doing what I really wanted to do, and I was in charge of the 'fancy department', as it was called, because of the scarves, belts and beautiful handkerchiefs. Old lady Beattie used to come, and she'd sit down at my counter and I'd get her a chair. She was such a dear old soul, no swank or pomp about them; they were lovely people.

When Mr James Beattie, the younger one, Jimmy, was there, he had a super twenty-first birthday party, up in what used to be the café restaurant, and we were all invited to that. There was a dance, a band and bowls of punch on the side, just help yourself. Some of them were paralytic I'm afraid. Not me, although I did wander out, and they found me on the settee in the furnishing department, naughty girl.

Clara Williams, born 1911

Butchers and Bakers

When I left school my mother got me a job as an errand boy for a butcher, Fieldhouse in Merry Hill, and then they came to Whitmore Reans, Great Hampton Street, but that didn't last long. Mother knew a bloke who worked for Tate's the butchers, and I got a job as an errand boy for Tate's in Park Village, delivering the meat, taking orders, and doing anything else. I used to scrub the shelves out. They were well known, the Tate's, they had market stalls. I was late one morning and Mr Tate said, 'I'm not having this, you're sacked.' They never knew what time I started, because I didn't go to the shop, I used to go to Marsh & Baxter's and get whatever they wanted there and then take it to the shop. I had already

done half an hour's work or more before I got to the shop.

Then I went to work for B.V. Wood, the service bakeries in Tettenhall Wood. I stopped at Wood's for quite a while, and he was quite upset when I left to go to Goodyear, for better wages, in 1934. You had got to be eighteen to work at Goodyear, and I started there on my birthday. I stopped there for eight years. It was a protected industry; they kept what blokes they wanted, but in 1942 I come off the list and so I went to Selman & Hill, an engineering firm in Church Lane, in the centre of Wolverhampton. Then I left them and came to Daimler. When the war started they had moved to the Courtaulds buildings from Coventry, and a lot of Coventry people came to live round here. My brother-in-law, Frank Head, got me that job. I was drilling, and we were making armoured cars. Then I was called up into the Navy, and I was in there three years.

After the war, much later, I went to work for the Ministry of Pensions and National Insurance in Bath Avenue; it was a bit different from being a butcher's errand boy! We used to have smashing annual sports days at Aldersley Stadium. I remember being in the sack race on one occasion. Happy days.

Percy Kyte, born 1916

Electric Construction Company

I started at the ECC in 1932. I did fifty years and finished in 1982. I actually did fifty years and three months. My father worked at the Great Western Railway's Stafford Road Works in the tender shop, as did my brothers Arthur and Griff. My sister worked in Courtaulds, and my other brothers, Frank, Horace and Cyril, worked at the ECC. As a boy I started at fourteen, and first of all I went in the switchgear department. I was an errand lad virtually, I used to go to the stores and fetch

Mr T. Bull and Mr S. Jones in the engine room at the ECC in 1917.

Ross D. Willcock at the Electric Construction Company in 1931.

the parts required by the men in the fitting area. From there I went alongside one of the men who made AC starters and DC starters. I worked alongside them, and I helped them to make these starters. I carried on for quite a number of years.

When the war came we had a big order for floodlight controls, and they wanted them out as soon as possible. We worked three days continuous, without coming home, we didn't even sleep. There was about eight of us and they kept bringing us food and sandwiches,

keeping us going. Eventually we got the order out in time, that was the main thing, and when we went home we slept for ages. That was the ECC: if you got a big order, you got it out as soon as possible. It really was a wonderful place to work.

I was called up in February 1943 and was an engine artificer in the Navy for three and a half years. I caught malaria when I was in Mombasa.

I later had an electrical shock at the ECC. I was disconnecting a transformer and the

The ECC hockey team in 1954. From left to right, back row: Stevens, Smith, Saunders, Churchward, Le Brocq, Barratt. Front row: Hollyhead, Pettinger, Benton, Gwilliam, Kay.

chap who connected it up put it straight on the mains, which I never did, I put a switch there and connected up dead wires. As I pulled the lead off it went round my hand, and I couldn't let go. I was bouncing up and down on the floor, and they said after I was squealing like a pig. A fellow in the stores ran up and knocked me off the lead, and I was alright then. They sent me home, and the doctor said I could come and see him in the morning, but I couldn't move, I couldn't move my arms, my hands, or my legs. It took several days before I could move again, but that cured my malaria.

Harry Jones, born 1917

Butler's Brewery

My Dad used to tell us stories about Butler's Brewery, that you wouldn't believe. He was in what they called the forwarding department, as a truck driver. One day he was taking an overload from the brewery to Shrewsbury. His pal Pongo Griffiths from Bilston was also a driver, but he was with my Dad as an extra drayman. Me Dad was poorly or something, and when they got to Shifnal, Pongo Griffiths got me Dad's hat and flung it through the window. My Dad said, 'What the soddin' hell did you do that for?' So he pulled up and got out to get his hat and when he got out Pongo slipped across to the driving seat and drove off. He shouted, 'We'll see you back here.' So they went and did the load and picked the old man up on the way back. He went in the pub while they were away.

Another time they were coming back from Shifnal or Wellington, and they came to the Junction pub in Kingswood. It was about four o'clock and one of the drayman said, 'Cor, I couldn't half do with a pint, pull up at the Junction, Aylie.' They called my Dad Aylie, I don't know why. The pub wasn't open, of course, so two drayman picked up an empty niner. They walked in the pub and they said, 'Here you are, landlord, here's your niner'. The landlord couldn't remember ordering it, but when they used to drop the beer the landlord would invariably say, 'I suppose you'll want a pint.' The driver used to have a drink

Springfield Brewery as it was in 1999, awaiting a new use.

Ron Tranter emerging from Springfield Brewery in 1960, long after the events described by Les Broadfield.

too. He wasn't supposed to; he got an extra five shillings a week or something so he wouldn't have a drink, but he did. The dray-man had a beer allowance at the brewery, two pints, but not the driver – he'd get the money for not drinking it.

They might make eleven or twelve drops a day, and they'd have a pint in every one. I used to go with them when I was a little one, and I've seen them. They would drop the beer and the publican would sign the ticket and then pull three pints and put them on the counter. They would drink them and then say, 'Well I suppose we'd better have another,' and pay for one. My old man used to drink at every pub, and at Christmas it was old ale. He could have perhaps twenty or twenty-five pints during the day. They used to pour it down.

They also used to have an allowance at the brewery, the draymen. Where the gates were at the brewery, on the left there used to be the Smacker Hole. There was a guy in there they used to call Smacker King, and they used to get their smackers there. The draymen were allowed two pints a day, at any time really, when they were in to have it.

One time I was with them and I used to sit in between my Dad and the drayman. I was about eight, and I used to sit on this little iron stump under the window where my Grandfather used to work. I used to get on board and the other draymen used to get on the back. This one drayman's name was Herbert, and he used to have what he called his kit with him: a little hammer, like a toffee hammer, and a length of rubber pipe. They would come out of the brewery and before they'd got to the end of Cambridge Street, he'd have the bung tapped out of a barrel, and he'd have a big black cider bottle, and he used to siphon the beer out. There was a vent in the cab, and he used to lift it up and call 'Aylie', and through would come a bottle, and there was a

shelf across the top of the cab, and my Dad would put the bottle up there, with a cork in it. Then Herbert would say, 'We'll have a drop of him from the Blue Boar'. There would be a row of these black cider bottles in the cab. They would have some out of every barrel.

On Sunday my Dad would go to the pub for a drink.

Les Broadfield, born 1925

Great Western Railway

I was sub-ganger on the Cosford stretch of line in 1926, and we were down to basic pay of £2 a week after the General Strike, and no Sundays and no overtime; not near enough to live on. We used to go rabbiting for the Blakemore's at Oaken Farm; Cock Meredith had the ferrets. They used to give us a shilling a couple, for all the rabbits we could catch. Of course we always managed to have one for the pot, and that's how we managed. We did manage better than a good many people.

The ganger in charge of the permanent way at Tettenhall, George Jeavons, lived on the Cannock Road, and he didn't like having to walk from the Cannock Road to Tettenhall every day, so when there was a vacancy on the main line at Oxley he applied for that, and I applied for his job, and got it, though the NUR was against me. Then they decided to do away with the passenger service through Tettenhall to reduce the wages bill. They did away with the stationmaster, three signalmen, three porters, a ganger, sub-ganger and a length man. I was ganger for the time being, then they brought into operation this motor-trolley system, and that extended the line from this side of Penn Halt to Baggeridge Junction. The ganger that was at Himley, Jack some-body, was senior to me, so I was asked to step back to sub-ganger. Jack was a man getting on in years, and he didn't want to be bothered

Dan Brew on his first ganger's trolley on the Tettenhall Line in the 1920s.

with these motor-trolleys. He had no more idea about them than I did at the start, I had to learn.

Before these motor-trolleys, you had to walk, pushing a hand trolley, flagging yourself. Then they brought this new system in which worked with a train stop, an electric token, when the signalman released the token to me, he'd given me possession of the line, but he couldn't let a train through, because he couldn't get a token out before I'd put mine in again somewhere else. The inspection trolley had a Douglas twin engine, and we also had a gang trolley.

Jack did not want to be bothered with all this so it was decided that after two or three months he would be given a job in Round Oak, and I would take over again as ganger. The first accident I encountered was before the motor-trolleys. I used to cycle down by the Mermaid at Wightwick, and get on the line at Lower Penn, then push my bike along

the track to say I'd walked it through. One day I was approaching the level crossing at Turner's Farm at Compton when the 4.50 from Crewe was coming towards me, whistle blowing, and the fireman leaning out and shouting, 'We've run through a flock of sheep there.'

He was quite right, he'd run through a flock of sheep on the girder bridge at Tettenhall. It was caused by people who used the canal for boating at weekends. They used to get their boats from a widow and her daughter who lived at the lock gate at Compton. Instead of closing the gate where there were sheep in the field at Turner's Farm, they left it open. The sheep naturally came over the bridge on to the towpath, then along to nearly Newbridge, where they had crossed the long field where a doctor kept his horses, and through a fifteen-inch-wide gap where they were putting a storm culvert in. They had got on the railway track and had slept on the bridge, some in the

Dan Brew on his last ganger's motorised trolley outside Wombourne signal box in 1957.

four foot [between the rails], some on the outside, and they'd got the rail for a pillow.

I wondered what the hell I could do, we had no communication, the station wasn't open, and the stationmaster, Pinfield, hadn't arrived. I had to walk to the branch box and advise the office what had happened. I said I'd try to find who they belonged to; some were dead, some were alive, some were wounded. I went back to Tettenhall Station and Pinfield had arrived. Turner at Compton used to have a milk delivery round, and just then his milk float went by. I told him what had happened and that these sheep must belong to his father.

I was that upset, I went to walk the fence to find out how they got in. Before I'd finished walking the fence Turner was there with a horse and cart, and motor lorry, and a

bloody great knife. Those that weren't quite dead, he killed them, and took them all straight to the abattoir. He only lost a few pounds. If he had left it, he'd have lost the lot, the company wouldn't have paid him.

Oh, then there was a suicide at Stourbridge Main Road Bridge. I'd pulled the trolley off at Wombourne, and there was a telephone message for me. 'There's a suspected suicide at Stourbridge Main Road Bridge. There's a man lying by the track with head injuries. You are to proceed to the spot and take a man with you for assistance.' So I went where the gang was working and asked for a volunteer with a shovel, and they said, 'For a start, what's the job, and what's the shovel for?'

I said, 'Well, there's a man lying with his head off, and the shovel's to clear away the oddments which are lying about. Who's coming?'

Nobody volunteered so I asked Harold, and he came with me. When we got there the policemen were already there, and they'd slid him down the batter to a waiting ambulance. There wasn't much of a mess. I asked what happened and they said, 'A very silly young man indeed, he'd fallen out with his young lady, a young man like him with all the wenches there are today. Lovesick, bloody forlorn, comes here and decides to finish it.'

There again they'd say he was of 'unsound mind', but never in the world. As he stood there in the stillness of the night, he could hear the train leave Wombourne, and hear it come down Himley Cutting to him. He could see a train coming from Baggeridge Junction right down the track. He'd got the nerve to put his head on the track and have it chopped off. Never insane, but it finished him.

Dan Brew, born 1892

Henry Meadows

When I left school I went to work for Henry Meadows in Park Lane, on a seven-year apprenticeship. I used to go to the Technical College as it was then, and they also did night classes in Springfield Road School. I had been interested in doing sign writing when I left school. I went to a place called Taylor's on the other side of town, I forget where. They used to have a place in Park Lane and then moved across town. They had a job doing up posh cars, painting them and that. The only sign writing I ever saw while I was there was one of Luce's the bakers vans. They put a big transfer of a cottage loaf on the side, and then the name over the top. I never did it, but I watched 'em doing it. I was most of the time in the pit, underneath cars, scraping the hoss shit off the bottom, while they was spraying

all round me. The smell of pear drops choked me, so I packed that in – at least my mother told me to pack it in.

After that I went to Meadows and became an apprentice. I went through the factory, through all the departments. I don't think I learned a great deal, but you had to do it, and I wanted to get into the drawing office, and eventually I got into the Jig and Tool Drawing Office. I finished the apprenticeship, from fourteen years old to twenty-one.

Meadows were mainly making gearboxes at the time. It was in the war of course and they made this huge gearbox, half the size of a room, for motor-torpedo boats. They used to put one of the Meadows engines into the gearbox on the test beds, and then test the gearbox more or less. Then they used to fetch them off and wheel them round to us in assembly to take apart. The bloody things were red hot, and I mean red hot. You could see them glowing and we used to burn our fingers. As apprentices we never realised what we was doing; we were just apprentices. We were just told to strip 'em down, so we did.

George Brazier, born 1927

Midland Metal Spinning

When I left school I became an apprentice at Midland Metal Spinning in Great Brickkiln Street. I worked mainly in the forgings place on the other side of the road in Pelham Street. It used to be the Clyno Cars factory, and you could still see the words 'Clyno' on the front of the factory. During the war it was taken over by De Havilland Aircraft. They made wooden aircraft, of course, like the Mosquito and the Airspeed Oxford. Airspeed had also been taken over by De Havilland. We made metal fuel tanks, Mosquito undercarriage doors, canopies, Oxford undercarriages, that sort of thing, in Brickkiln Street and Pelham

Street. Then when I was eighteen I had to go into the Army.

After the war I worked at Boulton Paul Aircraft, costing things like the Handley Page Herald wings, Beagle 206 wings, the extended Meteor wings, and one-offs like the Vintin amphibious car and a metal boat. Afterwards I was offered a job with British Aerospace at Stevenage, on missiles, and I worked there until I retired.

Bill Pauling, born 1927

Butler's Brewery

When I left school at fourteen I went to work at Butler's Brewery. I was living in Legge Street then, and I would wake at 4.30 a.m.,

Left The chimney at the former Clyno Cars factory in Pelham Street, later Midland Metal Spinning, being demolished in the 1980s.

Below An Airspeed Oxford aircraft, many parts for which were made at Midland Metal Spinning. This is the company aircraft of Boulton Paul Aircraft seen at Wolverhampton Airport in 1947.

without any call from anyone, and would be off to work at 4.45 a.m. walking all the way to Springfield where I would arrive at 5.45 a.m. I would sit in the mess room until 6.00 a.m., when we would start work.

One morning I was crossing the railway line on the Nineteen Steps (I never counted more than eighteen, though), when I heard the brewery clock chime three times. Thinking it odd I still carried on, and when I arrived at the brewery the gates were closed, and the lighted clock showed 3.10 a.m. I immediately started walking home, had a sleep on the sofa, and then started off to work again. I managed it correctly this time.

We had a ghost in the brewery, but that's another story.

Ben Owen, born 1923

Turner Engineering

I started work at Efandem, what is the Ever Ready now. I worked from eight in the morning to eight at night when I was fourteen, and for that I got ten shillings a week. I was covering the flashlights, sometimes in leather and sometimes paper, and fastening the snap-ups on the fasteners. I didn't like Efandem though; it was dirty work. I was there six months.

Then I worked at Turner's in Castle Street, opposite the Express and Star. During the war we used to make aeroplane springs for Rolls-Royce and everything. I could make a spring from start to finish. I never liked it there; I never liked factory work, but it was a case of having to. I was there for fourteen years, and I was earning twenty-two shillings a week when I finished to have my son. The Turner's were a family of three brothers and a sister. They really worked hard to build the business up but they were always falling out. The sister had a fruit shop on Snow Hill, Sage was her

Elsie Bradley on her wedding day in 1929, with her new husband Fred, who was employed at the *Express and Star*.

name. When the bosses called a meeting, I used to have to go to the shop and look after her children while she was at the meeting. I used to get sixpence for that.

I was married in 1929 when I was twenty-one. I met my husband, Fred Bradley, because he worked at the Express and Star on the despatch, which was on the other side of Castle Street. When I first went with him I was only sixteen; my father went mad, but I defied him. I got married at St Paul's on the Penn Road, my husband's parish; it's not there now. He was one of a family of twenty-four. His mother was an orphan and she got married at sixteen and died at sixty in Stafford Infirmary. She had three sets of twins, but she only raised nine of the twenty-four herself.

We went to live in Dawson Street, off Molineux Street. There was Red Cross Street, then Birchfield Street, then Dawson Street, where the John Ireland Stand at the Molineux is now. [Now the Steve Bull Stand – A.B.] I was a Wolves supporter for thirty-eight years. All the family went together; we went to Wembley twice.

Elsie Bradley, born 1908

Bakers Nursery

I went to work at Bakers at Codsall as soon as I left school in August 1934, 6.30 a.m. to 5.30 p.m., and to 1.00 p.m. on Saturdays, for ten shillings a week. My Dad got me the job; he went to see the manager of the place, a man called Moody, who was the spitting image of Adolf Hitler, and just about as frightening: his word was law. I worked in the glass department, I was there for eighteen months. I was told I was a bone idle young devil, and looking back on it I've no doubt they weren't far from the truth. Eventually, after a row with the glass foreman, a man named Cartwright, I put in a week's notice, and I learned afterwards that it was just about a week in front of the fact that I was going to get the bullet anyway. I was out of work for about five weeks, in weather that was snow and ice, and I spent most of my time skating on the pool on Kingswood Common.

Then I got myself a job in the nursery at Fallings Park. I couldn't even point to its situation now; it was only a small place. Then my Dad heard of a place in private service in Perton, again it has now disappeared. It was a large house and I was there twelve months or so. Then there was an opening at Beamish for an under-gardener under Fred Broom. I applied and got that, he knew me anyway, and there I stayed until I joined the Air Force.

John Brew, born 1922

Above The king and queen at Boulton Paul Aircraft in 1940, talking to Herbert Strictland, the Managing Director, with a row of Defiants in the background.

Opposite above Boulton Paul Aircraft employees with more than twenty-five years service. J.D. North, one of the great pioneers of British aviation, is central in the front row. Jack Chambers is sixth from the left, back row.

Opposite below Boulton Paul's Gorell Cup-winning football team, 1949.

Boulton Paul Aircraft

I went to work for Boulton Paul Aircraft when they moved to Wolverhampton from Norwich in 1936. The day I joined I remember seeing a man in a dirty old raincoat supervising the arrival of the Armament Drawing Office from Norwich; he was barking out his orders. I assumed he was one of the labourers, and I was shocked when I later discovered he was 'Pop' Hughes, the head of the armament department.

When the king and queen toured the factory in 1940, the door to the Tracing Office was 'conveniently' left open. One of the tracers was Cecile Clarke, the daughter of the chief designer, H.V. Clarke. When they came

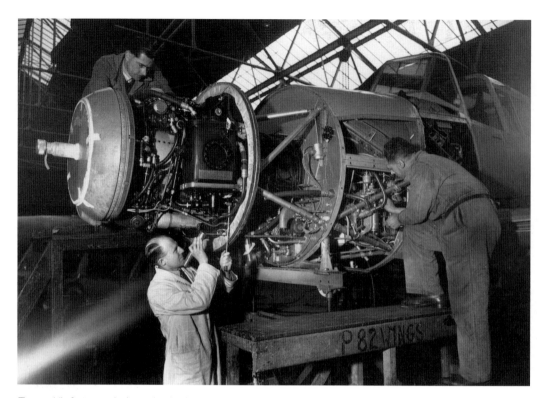

The world's first ever single-engined turbo-prop aircraft being assembled, the second prototype Boulton Paul Balliol T.1, late 1948.

to the Tracing Office, Cecile was introduced to the king by her father and Queen Elizabeth spoke to four or five of the other girls nearest the door. As there were about twenty girls in the office, there was a great deal of disappointment expressed by those who had not been introduced to their majesties, and much weeping afterwards.

With the outbreak of war the workforce swelled considerably and new buildings went up everywhere, all at government expense of course. One problem was to feed this army of people, and with the severe rationing at the time, the fact that the factory received an extra food allowance meant everyone took advantage of the canteen facilities. An extra canteen was built at the front of the factory and was used mainly by the staff. The original canteen was extended and a marquee was erected on spare ground near the boiler house to supply sandwiches and snacks. Pigs were kept as an extra supply of meat. They were tended by land girls and fed on swill made from scraps from the canteen. The girls also grew vegetables for the canteen.

After the war the canteen in front of the factory fell into disuse until there was a dispute with the sheet-metal workers, which caused the company to be 'blacked'. All the sheet-metal work was taken on by a small firm called E. W. Humphreys, which occupied the canteen. In the 1970s some of its former glory returned when it was converted to an executive canteen and became known as 'The Silver Grill'. It has now been demolished.

I worked for Boulton Paul for forty-seven years.

Jack Chambers, born 1920

Bayliss, Jones & Bayliss

I started working for Bayliss Jones & Bayliss in 1944 when I was fourteen, when I left Willenhall Road School. My Dad used to work for Baylisses, and my Grandad, and my aunts and uncles. Everyone round there worked for Baylisses in Steelhouse Lane, Monmore Green, and Rough Hills. People used to stay there all their life, fifty or even sixty years. They had long-service presentations every year, and there was usually someone who had put in sixty years' service. My Grandad worked there until he was seventy. He was only five foot tall; he was a blacksmith's striker and he wasn't much bigger than his hammer. There was a chap named Shay who was his blacksmith, and he used to say, 'When I nod me head, George, hit it.' It was an old joke.

My Dad worked there too; he used to be a nut-cutter. They took red hot bars, and what-

Above The staff of the power station at Bayliss, Jones & Bayliss, who generated all the electricity required in the factory at the beginning of the nineteenth century

Below The staff of Bayliss, Jones & Bayliss' hurdle shop around 1907.

Above Bayliss, Jones & Bayliss' clock tower, a prominent feature in Monmore Green for over a century.

Below Bayliss Jones & Bayliss made items from nuts and bolts to huge steel fabrications like this, leaving the works in 1955.

ever size nut they wanted, inch, or three-quarters. They used to take the white-hot bar and put them in a machine which shaped the nuts to whatever shape was required, and then there was a punch which punched the holes into the nut. There was a machine which used to cut the nut off the bar, as they fed it in. After a time the bar would get cold, and they had to put it back in the furnace, and start again. When they came to the end of the bar they used to get it with tongs, so they wouldn't waste any material, and feed the last bit in. He used to come home at night, and the soles of his feet were covered with blisters. The factory had a steel floor, and the heat of the furnace used to make it red hot.

I started off drilling Bailey bridges. There were holes at each end of the struts, and I drilled each end, some of them were ten or twelve feet long, an inch and a half of steel thick. I had to go in the Army when I was eighteen, but I didn't erect any Bailey bridges,

Above Presentation of long-service awards in Bayliss, Jones & Bayliss' canteen in 1954.

Below The Bayliss, Jones & Bayliss football team, who won the Division II Cup in the Wolverhampton Works League in 1956.

and when I came back when I was twenty I went back to Baylisses toolsetting. I worked on products like rib-washers, boss-fangs, as well as tines and other agricultural equipment.

My brother worked in the Cut and Punch, and my Dad was a nut-cutter. Another trade was the bolt-headers. They used to make the bolts which held the rails on for the railways. There was a line with the furnace at the top, then there would be a forger to put the top on, then another forger, then a stripper. They used to toss it to the next tray, and he'd stick it in a socket, pull it out, put it in the next one, to forge the top of the bolt; then he'd throw it to the chap next door, and he'd finish it off and put the stamp on, GWR or whatever it was; then the stripper would strip off the surplus material, and then the twister would put the thread on. Then the bolt would go down a tube to an iron barrow, and they would be stacked up in the barrow, red-hot iron. And there were two blokes; one was named Joe Mayer and one was named Ernie something, and they used to have to put a strap round their shoulders and take the bolts to where they had to be sorted, and they had the sweat pouring down their face.

They used to make parts for Fords, bumper arms and bumper brackets. They worked for the mines and the railways, and they made the iron steps for the telegraph poles.

The Press Shop where I worked was right on the canal, and there was only corrugated-iron walls, but half of the tins were down, and in the winter the snow used to come in, it drifted in on the steel bars. The tools used to be so cold, once you started using them they used to burst, so you had to go round and heat them up before you could use them. The furnaces were the only things which kept the place warm really.

Baylisses used to have their own barge on the canal. There was a chap named Ernie Webb, who used to pole it up the canal – they hadn't got a horse. They used to fill it with bolts and screws, and he used to take them up to the goods yard to be loaded on the trains, poling the barge, like they do on the canals in Venice. In 1947, when we had the big freeze, the cut was frozen for three months, from November to March, and they had to use the lorries then.

I used to play football for the Works League. They had a lovely pavilion, one of the first to have showers. They had two pitches at the ground, at the top of Steelhouse Lane. All the big firms had teams, E.P. Jenks, Courtaulds, Hobsons, Garringtons, Goodyear. One of the best teams was Marendelos, the ice cream people. They used to pay players to play for their team, give them backhanders. Of course the best team was always Goodyear: they had the American belief that their team had to win, and they used to give jobs to professional players. It didn't matter what they did in the factory, they could get more money than if they had been playing. [Like Bill Patterson of Cowdenbeath – A.B.]. Goodyear were always top of all the divisions.

Every year Percy Bayliss used to put a wreath on the plaque which commemorated the people who died in the war, and if you wanted to come to the service you could switch off your machine and go. Baylisses was a real happy place, a family firm. Then after they were taken over by GKN, they had a new regime come up from London and brought in new ideas, and they ruined the place.

They were just opening a new Fine Fare supermarket in Wednesfield, which is where I lived by then, and I went in there to ask if they had any jobs, and they made me assistant manager right away, even though I came straight from industry, but the job was at the other new place at Fallings Park. It became Gateway later, then Somerfield. I took a £6 drop in wages, three-quarters of my money, because I wanted to get away from Baylisses I was so fed up. Later on I rose to become manager of the Fine Fair in Bell Street. After that I went to Manders Paint as a supervisor of the tinters.

Doug Quinton, born 1930

The Culwell

I started at the Culwell in 1949, straight from school, fifteen years old. The Culwell was Joseph Evans' Culwell Works, in Woden

Joseph Evans children's Christmas party in the Culwell canteen. Geoff Bates is the older boy, centre right, looking down at his little sister.

Road, Heath Town. I went as an apprentice in the pattern shop. In those days the pattern shop was full, and they only took one apprentice a year, and they had already promised my father, who worked there, that they would have a place for me. So they found me a place in the fitting shop for three months, and then I was transferred to the pattern shop.

My father worked there for about thirty years. In the twenties he cycled all round Birmingham, Wolverhampton and the Black Country after a job. He lived in Bilston. When he started at the Culwell he worked one week on and one week off. Eventually things picked up, and he went on full time.

I started in 1949 and apprenticeships then went on until you were twenty-three years old, and you didn't get the full rate until you were twenty-three. You got quite a big increase when you were twenty-one, though no one in those days ever knew what other men got. It was secretive, and they didn't have a union then, so although they said you were offered the full rate, you were never sure you were getting the same as the guy next to you. When I was about twenty-one, the chaps on the shop floor put in for a substantial increase, which the management turned down. That is when all the shops joined the union, and the patternmakers union took up the case, but at the end of the day it meant the whole of the pattern shop had to leave. They were all sacked, which just left myself and I think about three or four other apprentices. We just carried on, and eventually a few other guys were employed. I remember one chap, an ex-

The interior of Joseph Evans & Sons giant Culwell works around 1902.

Brit, came over from Canada. He had retired at sixty. He heard that if he came to England he could get free teeth and free glasses on the new NHS. He came over and went to the Labour Exchange, and of course there were jobs going for patternmakers. The old ones never came back; we never saw them again.

We made all sorts of pumps, steam pumps, centrifugal pumps, ram-type pumps, air compressors. In those days, like a lot of companies, they made everything. They had their own drawing office, their own pattern shop, their own foundries, two grey iron foundries and a brass foundry, a machine shop and a fitting shop. There were very few things bought in in those days, even the studs that went in the flanges were made in-house. It was all on the one site, at the Culwell, which is now an industrial estate.

I used to play football for the Culwell; we used to put benches in the back of the works van and we all used to clamber in there. We used to get changed in the works canteen and then pile into the van and off to the venue, and then we used to come back to the canteen to get changed again. The home ground was Heath Town Park. After I left the Culwell, I played for Ettingshall Athletic, who are still going now.

I left when I was twenty-three. I had joined the union by this time, and I found out through the union that F.H. Lloyd of Wednesbury, which was a well-known steel foundry, had built a new pattern shop and were recruiting twenty-five patternmakers, and they were the highest-paid patternmakers in the Black Country, on a par with Birmingham; only Coventry got more. I got a job there, when they sent for me six months later.

Me Dad stayed at the Culwell until the company was bought by Pulsometer Pumps of Reading, and they sold it to Weirs of Glasgow and they closed it all down. Funnily enough my father got a job at F.H. Lloyd where I was working. When I worked there it was owned by the Evans family still, who lived in Tettenhall. Although old man Evans had got a Daimler in the garage at home, he never used it; he used to walk to the bus stop and catch a bus. There was a bus stop right at the top of the street, but he used to walk one stop further on, because it was a halfpenny cheaper. And then of course he would change buses in town and get one out to Heath Town. The interior of the Daimler was a dark maroon velvet, I remember, but when he got rid of it there was only something like 900 miles on the clock.

Geoff Bates, born 1934

West Central Garage

Just after the war I was working at Boulton Paul, and there was a man named Stan Smith who worked in the stores with us, and one day he said he'd been offered a job at Motor Services, but he was comfortable here and so he recommended that I go and see Mr Mallard, and I got the job. They were in Raby Street, they were Rootes Group distributors. Then there was a job offered to me at West Central, in School Street, opposite where Beatties car park is now. It was a big garage, but there's a row of shops there now. I was put in charge of the stores there. Next to the Methodist church there's an alley, and next to that was my stores, and then there was a big frontage for a show-room for the cars. I was very happy there, because I was me own gaffer. They were local distributors for the Rootes Group. The Rootes Group appointed distributors and gave them a discount and they appointed agents, and gave them a piece of the discount.

I learned to drive at West Central; they took me all over Wolverhampton. The com-pany bought a Ford 10 from a vicar at one of the churches in Chapel Ash; they paid £25. They overhauled it and then sold it to me for £90. It had rod-operated brakes.

One day the gaffer sold the business. He sold it to Attwoods, who were Vauxhall dealers. They also held Cyril Williams in Cleveland Street, opposite where Billinghams used to be. I went there, but I was no longer my own gaffer, because we had a big man down at Attwoods who took control of the lot. I day like that. One day a customer said to me, 'Yow aye very happy here are you John?' and I said, 'No.' He said that they had applied to him to get someone as a storeman in Heath Town. Well, I day know where Heath Town was. It appears he was a manager of the local labour exchange, this customer. It turned out the storeman job was at Manders Paints. I had my interview and I got the job.

John Clewlow, born 1912

Manders Paints and Inks

I was at Manders for sixteen years, very happy, a marvellous company to work for. It was a family company, and even the Chairman of the Directors at the time, Mr Phillip Mander, would come into my office and say, 'Hello John, how are you, how's things?'

In those days you never asked for a rise, and you never got a rise, but by moving from one place to another you got another pound a week. When I went to West Central in charge of the stores, I had been on £17 10s a week, but when I went to Manders I was on the same terms, but it was £14 plus £3 10s bonus. Eventually they amalgamated the two, which suited my purpose, because when you went on holidays you only got the £14. I spent many happy years at Manders.

I used to cycle each day from Tipton to Heath Town. Even when I worked at Austin

Aero at Longbridge I used to cycle from Tipton. We had a tandem, and when my eldest son was born we bought him a sidecar to go on the tandem, at £4 19s 6d. We were the talk of the district, wearing plus fours and a jacket, the cycling outfit of the time. We cycled all over, we cycled to Rhyl one time.

John Clewlow, born 1912

Dunstall pub

My mother's parents, Henry James and Elizabeth Darby, kept the Junction in Whitmore Reans. I'm not sure if it was the Junction Inn or the Junction Hotel. My Grandfather had a card printed which referred to it as the Junction Hotel, but we always referred to it as the Junction Inn.

My father's family lived further along Lowe Street; they had a paper shop. He was one of ten and he was an orphan when he was seven. He was the youngest, and his father died when he was three months old and his mother died when he was seven, and they all helped bring everybody up. When one left, the next oldest took over, and they ran the paper shop as well.

My Grandmother had three children, Harry, Vera and my mother. Vera was taken ill, so my Gran sent for the doctor, and you had to pay in those days so you did not easily send for a doctor. He came along and examined her and said she had appendicitis and that it was about to burst, and it needed an operation there and then. He asked Gran if she thought she was up to assisting. She said 'Yes' and the kitchen table was scrubbed down and they did the operation there and it was successful. My mother sat with Aunt Vera when she was recovering, but then she had a blood clot and there was nothing they could do about that, and she just died instantly.

Anne Surman, born 1940

John Thompson's

I worked for John Thompson's for fourteen years. They were a wonderful, caring, Christian family. People say they were the bad old days in many ways, and yes they were

The offices of John Thompson's in the 1920s. Only the central portion of this building still remains.

hard, but we just got on with it, and our characters were strengthened with determination to conquer whatever hardships came along, especially during the war.

The Thompsons involved themselves with the staff and working people, giving wonderful parties, with entertainment for all the children of the people, in the canteen, and they gave wonderful garden parties in the summer months to which all were invited.

At Christmas time Mr Pat Thompson used to arrive with huge bunches of holly and mistletoe to display around our offices, and on my seventeenth birthday he arrived with a huge bunch of sweet peas from the estate.

All the sons of the family started work on the shop floor in overalls, and only became directors when they knew everything from A to Z.

Marcelle Dovey

I worked for John Thompson's Boiler Works for forty years. We used to transport the huge boilers to Birkenhead Docks on long Scammell low-loaders. There were two drivers for each Scammell, one at the front and one at the back, operating the brakes; I was at the back. We only used to travel at 8mph, fully loaded, so I was able to jump off, buy some sandwiches, chase after it, and jump back on again!

Lawrence Smith

Ever Ready

I went to work at the Ever Ready in Lower Walsall Street in 1946. Before that I had been working in the Transport on Cleveland Road, doing the ticket boxes. We used to take the boxes the conductors had brought in from the night before. They were very cute, the conductors, they knew how to work a fiddle. We used to go through the numbers and work it all out. When the buses went to Walsall we had two lots of tickets; they had the one lot as far as the Walsall Line, and when they went over the border they had a different lot for the Walsall Transport, and they split the takings.

The Ever Ready used to be the AJS wireless factory, and there was one or two that had worked there making the wirelesses before the

The entrance to the Ever Ready works in Lower Walsall Street.

Above 'The Transport': the Cleveland Road bus depot in 1975, at the Bilston Road end.

Below Maud Price, supervisor, and Flossie Tooth, a torch welder, at the Ever Ready works, c. 1950.

war. I was only going to do two years, when I was married to get some money behind us. My husband worked at Rubery Owen, though he was a carpenter by trade. After three or four years I was put in charge of the band of girls making the front cycle lamp, which was made up from when it was a flat piece of metal. Each girl had a different job to do. Flossie Tooth was a welder, spot welding the boxes as they were folded, and the brackets were put on. Then they were put through the vats, and then there was a girl who used to spray them, then to the finishing line, which I was not in charge of at first, but when that lady retired I was put in charge of them too. We used to make 6,000 front lamps a week. Afterwards they went to plastic front lamps and the cases were bought in, so I took over the rubber torches, and over the other side of the shop I had a little band which did the red square lamp, a hand-held lamp with the big, square battery. There were only four girls on that. One of the inspectors was called Maud Price, one of the 'viewers' as we called them. She used to walk up and down the bands and pick a torch up off the band and look it over.

We made all sorts at the Ever Ready, pen-lighters, great big long torches for the police, and all the batteries came from the Park Lane works. Afterwards the black shop, where they made the batteries, came to Walsall Street, the first set of doors after the bridge. Then that closed down completely, even before I retired. They made Drydex batteries as well as Ever Ready. We made them with different names; all they used to do was change the stamp on the presses and people used to buy one name because they thought they were better than the other, but they were all the same really.

We didn't have a social club at the Ever Ready but we did start up a badminton club, in one of the shops at the factory. At the end of the day it all had to be cleared and we used to go back of a night time. I used to go home and have me tea, and then go back about seven o'clock.

After I'd done twenty-one years I had a watch, but we had to go to London for that. There was quite a crowd that went that year, when I went. It was marvellous what they put on. In all I did thirty-three and a half years at the Ever Ready, and it wasn't very long after I finished that it closed down. When I finished they presented me with a pink rubber torch, in a box. I've still got it in the attic. I enjoyed it there.

Lily Garbitt, born 1920

Coal merchants

After the war I went to work with my Dad for a while in his coal merchants, E.G. Kyte & Sons of Mill Lane; he was one of the sons, Percy, the same name as me. In those days by every road bridge over the canal there would be a coal merchant, because the coal was brought in by barge, usually from Cannock coalfield. There were coal wharfs at Hordern Road, Newbridge, Compton and Wightwick, and we were at Compton. The winter of 1946/47 was terrible, and there was a coun-trywide fuel shortage. The canals froze over and the snow lay on the ground for months.

Our barge was stranded at Cannock, unable to move because of the ice, then an ice-break-ing barge came through and my Dad decided to have a go at getting through. The profes-sional boatman were against it, and said we'd never make it, but we set off, with our horse, Paddy, pulling the barge. At every lock we had to lie on the towpath and clear away the lumps of ice from behind the lock gates with our hands, so they would open. The poor horse was slipping and sliding, and the snow built up under his hooves, so he was getting taller. We had to stop regularly to knock the snow off his feet.

Then Paddy slipped down an embankment and took me with him, how we weren't seri-ously hurt I'll never know. We managed to get him back up again, and we made it all the way to Compton. Then we had the problem of getting the coal to our customers on the lorry, as many of the roads were blocked with snow drifts. On the Pattingham road, where the road went through a dip on Perton ridge, there was a bus completely buried by snow, and people walked over the top of it without knowing it was there.

We were the first truck to make it through to the village of Trysull for some time, and on the way we came across a man who had cut down a tree for firewood. We threw the tree on top of the load, and carried it into the vil-lage for him.

Percy Kyte, born 1916

The Compton Road junction of the Staffs & Worcester Canal.

The interior of the Guy Bus bodies workshop.

Guy Motors

I started at Guy Motors around 1954, when I finished my service in the RAF, as a draughtsman on the Sunbeam trolley bus section. I had done my apprenticeship with Joseph Evans & Sons in the Culwell Works, starting around 1946, and when I finished my apprenticeship I did my National Service; I then signed up for three years. In the Culwell we made pumps, and I went right through, machine shop, fitting shop, drawing office, and served a proper apprenticeship.

When I got discharged from the RAF, I didn't go to the Labour Exchange, I went to the Sailors, Soldiers and Air Force Association, in Berry Street, and when I went, there was an ex-RAF man who was in charge. He interviewed me and sent me down to Guy Motors and I saw Doug Parnell, who was the Chief Draughtsman on the Sunbeam trolley

buses, and he gave me a job. Trevor Dudley was the Chief Draughtsman for Guys, and his two deputies were Howard Mallows and Gordon Evans. I was on trolley buses about nine years. The Bergen, Norway contract was the last contract in 1963. Prior to the Bergen contract they sold some to Johannesburg, South Africa. They sold trolley buses all over the world, places like Oporto. There were also Guy trolley buses, but all the time I was there I don't remember them doing any Guy trolley buses, they were all Sunbeams.

They made the trolley buses in what was known as the Gun Shop, at the very top of the factory, which, when I first went there, was where they were refurbishing ack-ack guns. The trolley buses were one side of the workshop and the anti-aircraft guns on the other side. When the trolley buses finished we went on to Guy work, buses and other vehicles. The drawing office was at the front of the factory on Park Lane. That building is still there now, about the only bit of the Guy factory left.

While I was there they made the Frisky motor car with Henry Meadows next door. They used to push the chassis through a hole in the wall and put the fibreglass bodies on in Guys. Then they'd go back to Meadows and their senior apprentices used to do the road testing. They used to go as far as the Pear Tree on the Cannock Road. It had four wheels but the back two were very close together; it had a Villiers two-stroke engine, I think. Wright's Garage on the Cannock Road used to sell them; they were the local agent.

We also put Henry Meadows' engines and gearboxes in Guy vehicles. They also made generators, which we had at the Culwell when I was an apprentice there. We had them to go on the pumps. They were used for Operation Pluto for pumping petrol under the Channel after D-Day. Meadows' generators with Culwell pumps. They also had Meadows engines in high-speed launches. Night time was the time they tested them, and the houses on the Cannock Road, where we lived, used to shake. One of the senior testers, a Mr Foster, lived about four doors down from my parents. He was a Merchant Navy engineer, and being as he'd got all his certificates for marine engines; he was a tester and the MOD inspector.

I had to leave Guys, with a good many more, when the company ran out of pennies with the Wulfrunian bus, and we were made redundant. They did not have the chance to develop it; one of the Ridings, East Riding or West Riding, in Yorkshire, bought the Wulfrunian, and the air suspension did not have enough money put into development. There were a couple of Wulfrunians running around in Wolverhampton, I couldn't tell you if the town actually bought them or whether they were loaned for development. Guy was taken over by Jaguar then, and I was a Jaguar employee for a short while.

It was alright working at Guys, the lads were alright. They had a decent social club and a good football team, and interdepartmental cricket matches and football matches, with their own playing fields in Park Lane, which is all built on now. While I was there Guy bought ABC Coupler, and that was the service department.

Also down Park Lane was the Ever Ready, the black shop. The girls all used to come out of there covered in black carbon from the batteries. You'd be educated too if you got on the bus with the Ever Ready wenches, with their language. People would cringe at some of the things they would be saying, the tales they would tell. The office staff from Guys, Meadows and ABC Coupler would try to get on the bus on the Cannock Road before the black shop wenches. They would literally run down Park Lane to get at the front of the queue, otherwise they'd stand back and let them get on first, both because of the language and the blackness. There was a chip shop on the Cannock Road, I think a family named Smith kept that, and the Ever Ready wenches would go in there for their chips, all black, and their fingers would be white by the time they finished eating their chips. One of the senior foremen there, who'd come up to open the Ever Ready from London, lived about five doors away from us, and he said he'd never let anyone else from his family work there.

Ray Simpson, born 1930

Chief test pilot

What happened was, during this period (August 1949) I was employed as a test pilot at Boscombe Down, and then Lindsay Neale

A.E. 'Ben' Gunn, chief test pilot at Boulton Paul Aircraft from 1949-65, in front of one of the many Canberras he test flew.

and his assistant Peter Tisshaw [Boulton Paul's test pilots – A.B.] had their Balliol crash at Coven. I was sent up as a temporary replacement and I took a look round Boulton Paul. There were a couple of De Havilland Hornet aircraft in the experimental shed: there was a Fairey Spearfish, which was the biggest single-engined aircraft ever, and the Gust-alleviation Lancaster tucked in a corner, and of course behind the black curtains was the Delta, and this tempted me slightly! And then eventually J.D. North said, 'How would you like to be my chief test pilot?' And I said, 'I think...' and he said, 'Well, think about it overnight.'

I came back the next day and I said, 'There's one problem. I probably won't be able to get out of the Air Force, because I'm on a permanent commission.' That's when I saw power at work.

He pressed a button and said to his secretary, 'Get me Leslie.' I didna know who Leslie was, but it was Air Commodore Leslie Isles, who was a rep in London – of course he'd retired. He said, 'I've got Flight Lieutenant Gunn here, get him out of the Air Force.' He handed the phone to me and I gave my service number, and by that afternoon I was out of the Air Force; that's how it was done.

Above Ben Gunn (right) with Dr S.C. Redshaw, chief designer, Boulton Paul Aircraft, in front of the P.111 Delta at the factory.

Left Ben Gunn opening the Boulton Paul Aircraft Heritage Project, with Boulton Paul Association Chairman, Cyril Plimmer, in October 1997.

The Air Force were not very pleased with the Air Ministry because they said, 'We have not seen Flight Lieutenant Gunn since we crossed the Rhine,' because I'd been shuttled away to Boscombe Down, you see, because I had more hours on Tempests than any other chap. So that was me doing a job at Boscombe, and then at the Empire Test Pilots School, and of course your salary is paid by the Air Ministry; and that was it, they made me the chief test pilot of Boulton Paul Aircraft, that was the start of it.

Above Ben Gunn being strapped into the P.111 before taxiing trials on Wolverhampton Airport's grass runways in 1951.

Below George 'Loopy' Dunworth, Boulton Paul test pilot, next to a Canberra.

J.D. North was a great man, an absolute genius. As Farnborough was to the Air Ministry, Boulton Paul was to the industry, because he was such a brain. They would say, 'Give it to J.D. North, he'll sort out the problem.' That's why we had such a mixture of aeroplanes. He was a shy man, but all-powerful, and he certainly knew what he was talking about.

We did taxiing trials on the P.111 Delta jet at Wolverhampton Airport. The nose wheel had a bald tyre, and it would shimmy when you went over tarmac or concrete, so we changed the tyre. We also tried out the braking parachute at Wolverhampton. I didna do the first flight of the P.111; it was an RAE project so it was taken to Boscombe Down, and they did several flights, then I took over. It was hypersensitive, you know, I mean it was ridiculous; a theoretical rate of roll of 560 degrees a second at 500 knots – now that's crazy! All you had to do to roll was to move the stick one inch and back again and you'd been round. You had to watch you didna disorientate yourself.

Also the cockpit was actually in the air intake, and the air used to come in through the pop rivets in the wall, and pin-pricked you all the way up your arm! And it was bloody cold!

We also got a lot of subcontract work from English Electric for Canberras, with special navigation devices and special cameras, and all sort of things like that. But we had to find a suitable airfield because Wolverhampton Airport was no good, being all grass, so we found Seighford near Stafford. The aircraft would be flown in and the noses taken off and brought by lorry down to the main factory at Pendeford, to be worked on. Then they would be put back on the aircraft and we would do the test flying. Johnny Power and George 'Loopy' Dunworth were my assistant test pilots on the Canberras.

Then the TSR-2 was cancelled, and English Electric wanted all the Canberra work for themselves, and that was the end of the Flight Test Section at Boulton Paul, and I went to work for Rover Gas Turbines.

A.E. 'Ben' Gunn, born 1923

Don Everall (Aviation) Ltd

I was employed at Wolverhampton Airport from 1961 to 1966 in the latter part of the Don Everall tenancy, as a general assistant in the Flight Office and in the Flying Club reception. I knew Eric Holden, the Airport Manager, quite well; he was a very pleasant man and very interesting when he could be persuaded to reminisce.

One of the aircraft based there was MacAlpine's Queen Air, before this they had a De Havilland Dove. Both aircraft were flown by Johnny Atkinson, who was one of those natural pilots, the kind who inhabit boys' adventure stories. MacAlpine's employed their own licensed engineer, Fred Kirk. He held a private pilot's licence, and flew as a second pilot on the Dove, which was permissible under the regulations at the time.

Wolverhampton had its fair share of business traffic, both fixed and rotary, and one important source was the racecourse. On race days there were frequent fast drops-offs and pick-ups of jockeys arriving for rides at Dunstall Park, and then going on to other meetings. Most of the top names passed through, including Lester Piggott. Among the show business personalities were Stan Stennet, Jimmy Edwards and Dick Emery. When Dick Emery was doing a season at the Grand, he would hire a club aircraft for a bit of relaxation.

There were a number of small private groups resident on the airfield. There were three dentists who jointly owned a Tiger Moth and a superb Cessna 172, and operated

Captain Johnny Atkinson (second left) about to give a pleasure flight in a Don Everall Aviation DC-3 to local scouts at Wolverhampton Airport.

Eric Holden, Wolverhampton Airport Manager, with two of his staff in front of the Pfalz D.111 replica on its way to Ireland to film The Blue Max.

A truly historic Dragon Rapide at Wolverhampton in the fifties. In July 1936, G-ACYR, when operated by Olley Air Services, had been chartered to transport the exiled General Franco from Las Palmas back to Spain, via Tetuan in Morocco, to command the Nationalist rebellion and spark the Spanish Civil War. It is now in the Museo del Aire in Madrid.

under the aptly titled 'Thirty Two Group'. There was also a group who owned the Druine Turbi, who were all, I believe, licensed engineers who worked for Hobsons, a very pleasant bunch.

I was on duty when another business aircraft, Boulton Paul's Airspeed Oxford, made its final departure. The Pfalz replica was another of those momentous moments. It arrived quite suddenly one late afternoon. It had no radio and no flight plan had been forwarded. Instead there was this sudden sight of a First World War silver biplane, with black crosses, swooping out of the sky and landing on the grass, a truly spine-tingling experience. It stayed a very short time, just sufficient for the pilot to refuel. It was going to Ireland to film The Blue Max. It was powered by a Gipsy Major engine, with a couple of extra dummy cylinders to simulate a Mercedes inline 6. The rocker cover bore an ominous warning: 'Oil rocker bearers every two hours'. I bet the pilot took the shortest possible route over the Irish Sea!

I had parted company with Wolverhampton Airport by the time of the Marsh Lane crash. It was a sad event, the Dove was a safe aircraft. Was there any need to close the airport? The continued expansion of Halfpenny Green [now Wolverhampton Business Airport – A.B.] shows the need persists, but I suppose in this modern age concrete seems preferable to grass. I doubt whether Halfpenny Green pilots see brown hares racing them down the runways though.

John Reohorn

five
At War

Ken Owen in the uniform of the Staffordshire Regiment, 1941.

Joining up, First World War

At the end of August or the beginning of September 1914 I went to the drill hall in Stafford Street to enlist. You see I had finished my Territorial Army career as a passed-out machine gunner and a good shot, and I thought I would walk straight in. The place was crowded with blokes, and a Sergeant wanted to know what I wanted. When I told him I wanted to enlist he made no further to do about it but asked if I had a good set of teeth. Well, I never had a good set; I was thrown off my bike when I was a lad and it knocked a gap in the front. I opened my mouth and he had a good look inside and said they couldn't possibly think of taking me, because, if I had to live on bully beef and biscuits, I'd starve.

I told him not to talk so damn soft. I had nothing to show, not a bit of paper or anything to show that I'd offered my services. I was annoyed and told him that the next time that I came to see him, that he wouldn't trouble whether I had a head on or not, and that was it.

I got a job working for Banks Brewery, working on the drays, until March 1915. Then I had an accident with my finger, when I got it caught under a hogshead, and I was off on the sick. After a week I got fidgety, and

my bosom pal, Charlie, had gone in the Staffs Yeomanry. I went down Broad Street and they were recruiting for the 175th Staffordshire Brigade of Artillery. So I went in and told them I had thought of joining the Fusiliers, and they said, 'No, come into the brigade.'

I thought I should have to go through a riding school, but they said I was too big for a driver; I would be a gunner, so I consented. There were about thirty of us and we were told to go upstairs and take everything off. We formed a circle, stripped naked. This doctor come round and stood in the middle, I was behind him. 'Put your hands above your heads, move your fingers, move your toes.' He looked right round, no eye test, no stethoscope or nothing. He came round to me, and I had a finger stall on because the finger was touchy. He had me take it off, and I had to come back for another examination. I was then told to attend the recruiting office every other day until it was right. I think it was fifteen days, then he gave me my papers.

I went to train in Smethwick in April 1915, and we were there six or seven weeks, because while we were there the horses came. The major part of the brigade had been recruited in Nottingham, only the ammunition train came from Wolverhampton. We got issued with uniform a bit at a time. There was no

Dan Brew (second left, back row) as a military policeman, shortly after joining the Army in 1915.

beds provided, we had to sleep on the floor. There was a big pleasure gardens there, and the instructors had us running round the walks and leapfrogging, then into the hall and doing physical jerks.

The batteries had got no horses, they came to Hockley and we had to go up there to meet these horses. They were in cattle trucks with head collars on and a halter, they'd been ridden but I don't think they'd had any harness on. Well, you can imagine what it was like when we got into the streets with tram cars and motor cars, they were on the pavements and everywhere.

I hung back because I was used to handling some of those gentlemen, all the others who'd worked in factories had never seen a horse before; they were anxious to have a horse, you see, one horse, one man. I kept out of it, and walked behind and saw the antics. I expected one or two to go through shop windows, but they didn't.

We were billeted in the Town Hall at Smethwick, in a big yard at the back. There was a big boozer on the corner, just away from it, called the Blue Gate. Well, down the road there lead to some fields, that was where the horses were put on picket lines and sorted into batteries, and the drivers were selected. They got used

to having harnesses, but I had nothing to do with it. I was invited to be a garrison military policeman, which suited me at the time.

A bloke had deserted, and he was captured in Epping Forest. He was a deserter from the Warwicks as well. A bombardier and I were detailed to go and escort this bloke from Epping Forest. We'd brought him to New Street Station, and we had to wait for a train to Smethwick, so we went into a boozer over the road for a pint, and the bombardier treated this bloke to half a pint. After a while he said he wanted to go to the lavatory, and said, 'My word of honour, I'll come back.' The bombardier allowed him to go, and you can guess what happened. He was a Brummie, and he never came back.

When we got back to Smethwick Town Hall, the Adjutant asked where our prisoner was, and we had to say we'd lost him. We were placed under arrest, the pair of us. The Provo Sergeant heard what was going on, and he told us that the bloke would never be seen again, and that we should make up a tale between us and stick to it, so that's what we did. We told the Colonel next morning that the platform had been crowded and the man had slipped away and got lost in the crowds.

In the meantime the bloke had been arrested by the civil police and had had a different tale to tell. He told them he'd been taken to a boozer and given a drink, and had been refused permission to go to the lavatory, but he had slipped away through the lavatory while we were drinking. I was boiling, I went to the guardroom, which was in some schools, and asked to be let in. There was a room full of blokes and chummy was sitting on the floor. I went to him and gave him a real rollicking. I called him a lousy bastard. He jumped up and asked the bombardier if he had heard what I said, and the bombardier said he had.

The next day we were up before the Colonel, this time to answer a charge of assault, and chummy told his tale. The Adjutant said, 'I don't know the true facts of this case, but I imagine it goes something like this. They treated you like a gentleman, they took you into a pub, they treated you to a beer, and you gave your word of honour you'd come back, and you didn't. If I'd been in the position of that gunner, I shouldn't have stopped at calling you a louse-bound bastard, I'd have knocked your bloody head off!'

So I was very pleased with the result.

Dan Brew, born 1892

John Brew in County Lane, Kingswood, about the time he went to town to join the RAF in 1939.

Tragedy at home

I well remember the First World War. I was six years old when the war started; my father enlisted in 1915 and left my mother with six children, on ten shillings a week. During that time I had a sister burnt to death. My father was home on forty-eight hours leave at the time. He was stationed in Glasgow and he had gone for a walk around on the Monday morning; he was going back in the afternoon. My mother went to the shop just below, only 100 yards away, to fetch some bread and she left me two sisters playing in the kitchen. When she came back she could hear them screaming. She dropped her bread on the garden path and found my sister Florrie all in flames. My mother burnt all her arms.

There were neighbours standing about outside, and they said they thought it was children fighting. Florrie burnt to death; she was four years old. It was a terrible time.

Elsie Bradley, born 1908

Joining up, Second World War

Much against my Dad's wishes, in April 1940 I announced out of the blue that I was going up to Snow Hill to join up. I was frightened to death that the war would be over before I could do my share. There were two recruiting offices, the Army was downstairs and the Air Force was upstairs.

I presented myself downstairs with quite a bunch of other young gentlemen. A Colour Sergeant circulating around comes to me and asks what I was volunteering for. I said I was going to volunteer for the Tank Corps in the hope of catching up my mate. 'How old are you?' I told him I was nineteen.

'Sorry, lad, at present we've got as many volunteers as we can cope with, and we're not accepting anyone under twenty. If you'd like to go upstairs to the Air Force, they're still accepting volunteers from nineteen.'

I was that thick that I hadn't got the sense to go out into town, have my dinner, and come back in the afternoon aged twenty. I went straight up the stairs. 'Come in, sign here, and be back this afternoon for a medical.' At just after two they announced that I was fit, and I'd be sent for when I was required.

A week or two later I thought I was on my way. There came a travel warrant and a call-up paper to go to Cardington. All it was, we were actually enrolled, sworn in, given a more elaborate medical, and then given a little badge, RAFVR, and then we were all sent home on deferred service. I was deferred until August 1940. The badge was just to show folks you were waiting for call up and were in reserve.

John Brew, born 1920

Boulton Paul's Home Guard

Just before the war I went to work at Austin Aero in Birmingham. We were making the Fairey Battle, and after the Fairey Battle was finished we were making the Lancaster. I was in the stores. My brother got me the job, he was four years older than me, and he said he would get me transferred to his department, but Austin Aero stopped transfers. Then things went quiet and I saw a job advertised at Boulton Paul's, applied for the job and got it.

I eventually joined the Home Guard. They had a Sergeant Major there, I think his name was Northwaite, and he used to live in a pub in Claregate. He was an ex-naval man, and he used to stand on the flight apron. He would stand at one end and we stood at the other, and we had to shout at him, to teach us to use our voices. We learned to use the rifle and the Sten gun, and we used Boulton Paul's own ranges which they had for testing their gun turrets.

On one occasion they had a Halifax arrive down there to have the gun turrets fitted. One of us had to turn up at work in uniform, and I had the 'honour' of guarding this Halifax. It was a big thing.

One Sunday morning we had to attack an ack-ack gun site at Coven. I had my squad with me; I was a sergeant, and being a townie I didn't know anything about the countryside. There was this hedge with a little mound and a nice, flat, green area in front of it. 'Come on chaps,' I said, 'down behind it.'

I didn't know it was a slurry pit. I sank up to my waist in cow shit. They had to pull me out with a rifle, I was covered with it, waist down. It was raining, and the rain was still

The Boulton Paul Home Guard in October 1944, the stand-down parade.

coming down the spouts at the farmhouse nearby, so I had to stand under there to swill some of the mess off. We gave up the attack. Fortunately I had come to Boulton Paul's on my bike, and so I did not have to go home on public transport.

When I got home the wife said, 'Blimey, you stink!' But she never liked the Home Guard. She said, 'I can't see why you call it the Home Guard, because you're never at home.'

Once I remember attacking Weston Park, and walking back to Boulton Paul and getting lost. We had to phone Boulton Paul, and they asked for a map reference. Well, I day know where we were so how could I give a map reference? We had to walk back to Boulton Paul, and then I had to cycle home to Tipton.

On the top of the factory was a lookout and we saw Coventry being bombed from there. They let us go up and have a look. It was that close and that vivid I thought it was Birmingham being bombed, but it was Coventry. You could see the glow and you could actually see the bombs burst.

Just before the war ended I was called up. I was thirty-two at the time, which was a bit old. I did a couple of years in the Army.

John Clewlow, born 1912

Italian milkmen

I was born in Shifnal but we moved to Wolverhampton in 1939 when I was ten. We moved to Woodland Crescent, Merry Hill, just off the Trysull Road. It was a new estate; they were still building the houses, and they didn't finish them until after the war – they didn't even lay the road until after the war. There were still fields behind us. After the war they built more and more estates on the fields. My father got a job as Transport Manager with the Imperial Dairy, in Merry Hill at the top of Woodland Road. He was in charge of the heavy transport, bringing the milk in from places like Minsterley and Knighton. During the war he actually had to do some driving, because they couldn't get the drivers, they had been drafted into the forces. Consequently I used to go out with him an awful lot and, even though I was only a teenager, I used to take other drivers out to show them the round.

One time we actually had Italian prisoners of war driving for us, and I used to take them round to all the farms. They spoke not bad English. They used to come in from Cannock way, very early in the morning, sometimes on the back of a lorry. They worked for Midland Counties Dairy as well, and they used to deliver the milk. They had patches on their legs and on their backs, to show they were POWs.

My father did some work for the Ministry, because he was qualified on an articulated wagon, and he used to teach drivers from Halfpenny Green and Cosford how to drive Queen Mary's. He also did fire-watching. At the bottom of our road was an ARP post, and a chap named Harold Green and myself became runners for them. There was only one bombing raid in the area, and they bombed the playing field we used to use sometimes depending which school I was at, though we only might have one game of football in a month. My mother was drafted during the war, and had to go filling shells in Courtaulds, she couldn't get out of it. I got rheumatic fever and I had to stay in bed, and an aunt who lived in Blackburn Avenue, in Claregate, had to catch two buses out to Merry Hill, to give me my dinner. Later my mother was able to move to the dairy, though that was also a restricted occupation.

I went to various schools – Bingley Street, Graisley, Brickkiln Street – because there was a shortage of teachers, and I ended up at

Wulfrun College doing all my exams. When I left school I went to work as an apprentice for John Nicholls, carpenters and joinery, on the Birmingham Road. They had a box-making shop and a joinery shop. Then after my National Service, in the Far East, I came home and joined Boulton Paul Aircraft.

The Imperial Dairy is gone now; they pulled it down and built an estate of houses on the site.

Geoff Phazey, born 1929

Women war workers

My teenage years were taken up by the war, when there was food rationing and clothes coupons. I never had the lovely clothes that can be bought today. We were allocated twenty coupons, which had to last a year. You had to give eighteen for a coat, shoes were seven, a dress was seven, so you could not have bought many even if the clothes were in the shops. I used to rub wet sand on my legs, and when it was dry I would rub the grains off, and my legs looked tanned as if I had stockings on.

I worked in a war factory, Fischer Bearings, working nights as well as days, twelve- hour shifts, and five hours on a Saturday morning, and we only had one week's holiday a year and six odd days at Christmas and Easter. I travelled home alone through pitch-dark streets, for there were no street lights owing to the war. The only lights were tiny crosses on traffic lights, and cars only had side lights, which were turned off if there was an air raid.

I remember going home from work one dark evening, walking down Queen Street. It was pouring with rain, and when I came to the edge of the pavement my shoe came off. There I was, hopping around on one foot, trying to find it, feeling with my toe. With the blackout it was impossible to see the pavement. Lots of workers on their way home were passing me by, probably wondering what I was doing. I never did find my shoe, I had to go the rest of the journey with a cold, wet foot. I did wonder what the other passengers on the bus thought when I got on. When I got home my mother could not stop laughing, but I did not see the funny side at all. On the way to work next morning, there was my shoe, sitting on a wall about thirty yards from where I lost it; it was full of rainwater. It must have been kicked along by a pedestrian and someone put it on the wall.

When the air-raid sirens sounded we would get up in the night from our warm beds and go to the air-raid shelter, everyone had one in their garden. I would grab my case, which contained my shoes and what little clothing I had. This gave my parents much amusement, but I did not intend to be left with just my night clothes if the house was bombed. There were searchlights everywhere, criss-crossing the sky; it lit up the garden, and I was always relieved when I had run as far as the very large cherry tree that we had in our garden, for I always thought that the enemy pilots might not be able to see me, although I had to do another sprint to get to the shelter.

My father, Walter Pritchard, was an ARP warden, and after he had seen us safely to the shelter, he would go to his post at ARP headquarters up Caledonia Road, and he would be sent to where the bombing was heaviest. Sometimes we would not see him again for two days. One night three bombs landed sixty yards from our shelter, and when we climbed out of our dug-out we were shocked to see how close they were. There were craters in the road, including a big one at the bottom of Coventry Street right in the Willenhall Road. Two small ones dropped in St Giles Crescent. In the morning the buses from Willenhall emptied on one side of the crater, and the people walked round to get on another bus on the other side. I always managed to get on and get a seat before they arrived, where prior to this I was often left at the stop, as the bus was full and passed by.

We had no water or electricity as the wires were down and the pipes broken. We carried water from a supply brought to the Willenhall Road. The night the bombs dropped my father stopped in Coventry Street to help get the people out of the air-raid shelter. The people who had died were in the sloping doorway of the shelter. He put his coat on one person lying on a stretcher. When it was over he patted his pocket for his pipe, but it was in the pocket on its way to the hospital, much to his annoyance. He never got it back.

Leah Brew, born 1925

Bomber pilot

My brother Jack became a Whitley bomber pilot during the war. We lived with our parents John and Louie Owen, and sister Nora, in Deansfield Road. Jack went to Wolverhampton Grammar School and then got a job in the GWR offices on the Stafford Road. Our cousin, Ben Owen, joined the Army and was eventually part of Popski's Private Army, a behind-the-lines unit in North Africa and Italy. Another cousin, Ken Owen, joined the Staffords. Jack went to join up with his friends Billy Adams, who became ground crew, and Jack Whitehouse, who failed the medical.

He learned to fly at RAF Shawbury, and did his advanced training on Oxfords at RAF Abingdon. He was posted to No. 10 Squadron flying Whitleys at RAF Leeming in Yorkshire and flew about ten bombing missions over Europe. On returning from one of them they had to ditch in the North Sea, but were rescued by launch and taken to Grimsby. They

were taken to the best hotel in town for breakfast, dripping seawater all over the nice floors. They were rather put out when they received a bill from the hotel for the breakfast some time later!

In November 1941 he was posted to No. 138 Squadron, the cloak and dagger unit at RAF Tempsford who dropped agents into France and Holland and supplies to the Resistance. On his thirty-third mission Jack was searching for a drop zone at low altitude over Normandy when they hit a hill. He and three of his crew died and are buried in the churchyard at Vire.

Freddie Owen

Ken Owen in the uniform of the Staffordshire Regiment, 1941.

Jack Owen among the ninety-four officers and men of No. 10 Squadron at Leeming in 1941. Over the next month, twenty-eight of these died or became POWs, and the Whitley behind them was also lost!

First aid man

During the war I was a first aid man, three years in the St John's Ambulance. We used to go to Park Lane Bus Depot every night of the week and work. If there was a call-out for an accident on the street we used to go. We had two ambulances. There were a lot of accidents because of the blackout. One of the first ones I went to was down at Fordhouses. They put smoke boxes all the way along Stafford Road, right down to Boulton Paul. This smoke went up when there was a raid. There was this fellow who was walking along the middle of Stafford Road and he was run over by a lorry; the wheels went over him twice. He was in a

dreadful state; it was one of the worst sights I've seen. The lorry couldn't see him because of the smoke, I should think that was the reason he was hit.

We also had a lot of incendiaries dropped at Wednesfield, and we were sent out there in case people were getting hurt. I can remember the German plane which dropped bombs on Boulton Paul. He was that low we could see the pilot in the cockpit. We were at the top of Elston Hall Lane, in Bushbury, coming down to my mother's in Shaw Road for our tea, and he flew over so low you felt as if you could touch him. We could see the bombs drop, and the tracer shells from the guns in the

woods at Pendeford going over our heads. This was about half past six one Sunday afternoon. My wife's father was in the bath, and he jumped out and slipped and hurt himself. I'll never forget it.

Harry Jones, born 1917

RAF Perton

I arrived at RAF Perton in June 1942. It was a satellite of RAF Tern Hill and No. 5 Flying Training School. The aircraft used were Miles Masters, used for advanced flying training. Perton was the first airfield to be fitted with a mobile 'Mercury Sodium' type flare path, which I used to operate and maintain.

Perton was used as an emergency landing field and numerous aircraft paid visits,

Wellingtons, Hurricanes, Spitfires and a US Flying Fortress and Dakota. In October 1943 a De Havilland Rapide twin-engined aircraft landed and out stepped two smartly dressed RAF police sergeants, armed with pistols, and they asked us which airfield this was. When we told them 'Perton' they said, 'Never heard of it. Show us on the map.' While we were doing so a gentleman stepped out of the aircraft. He was dressed in a morning suit with a hat. He asked us our names and said, 'Nice to meet you, men. I am Sir Archibald Sinclair, the Air Minister.' A few minutes later they took off.

In June 1942 our aircraft were flying from the dispersal from the top end of the airfield near to the rear entrance which lead to Tettenhall Road, when a US Army jeep arrived at the closed gates. The driver and passenger, who was wearing a leather jacket and showing 'no rank', asked for admittance as they wanted to see the officer in charge of flying. They were allowed on to the airfield after the CO had talked to them. Shortly afterwards the ground crew were instructed to prepare a Master III for flight. I signed Form 700 for electrics and shortly afterwards the aircraft took off. The jeep left the airfield a few minutes later. The timekeeper came running out of his office clutching the Time and Flight Form, and in the passenger column was signed 'Clark, Mark – Rank: General'. Not long after that he was on operations in Italy.

During my stay at Perton very few crashes occurred. Only one was serious, when a Master III's engine blew up as it was taking off over the trees surrounding the Dutch Camp next door. The aircraft lost height and at that time appeared to have crashed in the Dutch Camp itself. The Fire Crew dashed to the area (I was with the unit) and shortly after found the aircraft on its nose in a ploughed field, just beyond the camp proper. The pilot was waving his arms about when we arrived, but was unhurt. After spraying the aircraft with foam, we took the pilot back to dispersal. He demanded another aircraft at once.

In July 1942 the Miles Masters returned to Tern Hill, then in September 1942 Perton was opened up again as a satellite of RAF Shawbury, with twin-engined Airspeed Oxford advanced trainers. I was posted away in January 1945.

Ken Jones, born 1920

The Princess Irene Brigade

By order and expense of the Dutch Government, a camp was built next to RAF Perton to house the Royal Netherlands Brigade 'Princess Irene'. After VE Day the camp accommodated the EM, or Expeditionary

Private A. Kramer of the Princess Irene Brigade of the Dutch Army, at camp in Wrottesley Park just after the war.

Force intended for the Far East and trained in the British Army.

I was in the camp, then named Wrottesley Park. I was there from 1945 to 1947, and it was a very good time to be there. I was one of the youngest, just eighteen years old and learning to cook.

A. Kramer, born 1927

Bombing

The men who worked with me on the railway had to go away at times; there was damage to be repaired everywhere. They were often away, but I had to stay on the job. I didn't have to do fire-watching or Home Guard; I wasn't allowed to do anything like that. I was to be kept entirely free to supervise my nine-mile railway. I was well satisfied with what I'd seen in the First World War; I didn't want to be bothered by any more.

When the Second World War started, the wife wanted an air-raid shelter, so I built her one in the garden with a couple of bunks in it and a candle and a tea pot. She said, 'They'll make a beeline for that ash tree there.' I said, 'The Lord Almighty, the thousands of ash trees they'll come over! What makes you think they'll make a beeline for that one?' But she'd got it firmly into her head that that's where they would come. Then she never went into the shelter; she stayed in bed, same as the other buggers who said, 'They won't bomb here'. They went to bed, and I was the only one who used to come out if there were alarms.

If there was alarms I would go out, and a time or two I stood at the end of the house (in Kingswood) by the chimney, listening to those bombers. One morning, in the early hours, I was out and they came for Cosford Airfield, and sprayed fire-bombs all about, some were this side of Albrighton, in the fields. As I stood I heard this plane coming and it seemed it was following the main road. A few seconds later there was 'Thump, thump!' and I thought that's between here and Tettenhall by the sound of it.

When I went to work on my bike in the morning, there was a policeman at Woodthorne Avenue and there was a traffic diversion. A bomb had dropped right by where the Ministry of Agriculture and Fisheries later was, he'd dropped a bomb right in the middle of the road and it took out the whole road. I went round by Woodthorne Avenue and turned left to the bus terminus. When I got in Tettenhall Station yard all the curtains in all the houses facing Compton were flapping through, it had blown the windows out.

One Sunday afternoon, when they were all in church, I walked up Kingswood Common, by the red house owned by the Hodgkisses. A big plane flew over, very low, and I looked up and there were bloody great German crosses on it. A few seconds later it was 'Bump, bump!', he'd made a beeline straight for

Dan Brew at his garden gate in Kingswood, from where he used to watch air raids at night during the Second World War.

Boulton Paul's. He missed and the bombs dropped somewhere in the fields. If you'd have seen them coming out of Kingswood Church! They were in one hell of a hurry, they never said no more prayers that night!

Dan Brew, born 1892

A Spitfire crash and the Humpshire Lancer

One foggy Sunday morning near the end of the war I was cycling along Marsh Lane by the airport, going to a riding stable near Codsall Church. I could hear the familiar sound of a Merlin engine, circling above, but could see nothing because of the thick fog. I heard the aircraft approaching and then there was an almighty crashing/crushing sound just ahead followed by dead silence; the sort of total silence only a mist can give. I cycled on a few score yards and came to a place where the hedges on both sides of the road and the iron railings on the airport side were all damaged.

When I returned later in the day, the mist had lifted, and there on the other side of the fence was a Spitfire in a very sorry condition. If I had cycled a little faster that day, it would have hit me!

I had started with Boulton Paul at the beginning of the war as an apprentice, and moved to the tool drawing office. One of the draughtsman was George Barratt – two As, two Rs, two Ts – as George used to say, to avoid confusion with a shoe advertisement of the same name. George was a real character and very old for a draughtsman. He was of slim build, medium height, and had wispy grey hair, gold-rimmed specs, and he always seemed to wear grey flannels and a reddy-brown tweed jacket.

George used to have a nap most afternoons. He laid his duster on the drawing board, put his elbows on the duster to prevent them from slipping, cupped his chin in his hands, and assumed an air of deep concentration.

George was the one who named the Humpshire Lancer, which arrived every night just before blackout time. He was christened by George because he was an old man with a humped back and he came from Willenhall, also known as Humpshire. Everyone in Willenhall made locks and keys, and were constantly bending over a vice, hence the humped backs. This was also why it was said that Willenhall pubs had holes in the walls behind the benches, to accommodate the humps.

The Lancer part came from the fact that he carried a long steel rod – needless to say a wary eye was kept on his activities. At one end of the 'lance' was a hook, the other end being a crank, like the crank handle of a car. Close to the ridge of the roof were fanlights which could be opened and closed by actuating a threaded rod, on the lower end of which was an eye. The hook of the 'lance' was engaged in the eye, and then turned by means of the handle. The fanlights had to be closed so that no light escaped through the open portion, to preserve the blackout, the glass being painted.

After the war the paint proved too hard to remove, so the painted glass panels were replaced by clear glass. The gang on the roof dropped a pane, which I well remember as it landed on the drawing table next to me, sharp edge down!

Bob Mee, born 1922

The Wolves in wartime

I first watched the Wolves in 1943 when I was nine years old, Wolves v Walsall. They used to play away one week, and at home the next against the same team. They had beaten Walsall 3-1 at Fellows Park, and then I saw them draw 1-1 at Molineux. The old South Bank was all fenced off. The area under the roof had a chain-link fence in front of it and was used for storage. The Wolves team used to change every week, because a lot of the players were in the forces. Wolves were lucky because they had RAF Cosford very close, and Lichfield Barracks, so they pulled a lot of players in from those places, who were on the books of other clubs. They could have a good team one week and a poor team the next week. They had a lot of internationals playing for them.

My uncle lived in Himley Crescent, Goldthorn Park, and Cyril Sidlow, the Welsh international goalkeeper, lived in the house next door, and Bert Williams lived across the road, so he had both Wolves goalkeepers living right by him. Consequently I used to get all the autographs from all the internationals.

Geoff Bates, born 1934

six

Shopping

Peter Brew meeting Father Christmas in Beatties store in 1953

Central Arcade

When I was two or three I got myself a horse from Millers the toy shop, or Sherwood & Morris, in the Central Arcade. We were walking through and it was standing outside. It was on wheels, and I just caught hold of it and walked. They were reaching the top of the arcade when they found out I had got a horse. They took it back. I don't think I cried though.

Percy Kyte, born 1916

Barnet & Jones

I left school just before Christmas 1934, and by New Year's Day I was working in Barnet & Jones in Tettenhall. We sold anything and everything. The shop, which was in High Street, was Carousel later on. Mr Barnet was the old chap and Mr Jones was his son-in-law. I was paid five shillings a week and out of that I paid sixpence a week off my bike. We used to close the shop for dinnertime, from one o'clock to ten past two, and one of the bakers, Mr Gaunt, used to give me a lift home on his motorbike. I was terrified on that motorbike, I didn't like it at all, so Mom said you shall have a bike, get what you want from Mr Adey's.

One side of the shop we had all sorts of hardware, wire netting, dustbins, you name it, corn for pigs and ducks, every sort of food for animals. I used to hate it if anyone wanted wire netting as we had to get it out on the pavement to measure it and to cut it. We used to sell a lot of wire netting, but I hated it.

The other side was all the grocery and biscuits. We used to have to weigh everything, there was nothing in packets in those days. On Mondays and Tuesdays, all morning you were cleaning the shop, cleaning the marble slab where we kept the butter, which was loose. You had to weigh that as people wanted it. You used to have to weigh sugar, flour, dried fruit, tea – Mr Barnet used to blend special blends of tea. We used to have to weigh pepper and we used to have to cut the salt into blocks. At the back of the shop we kept the butter, cheese and lard and all that in big tubs, to keep it cold on the stone floor. There were no freezers or fridges.

Mr Barnet was a little old man, a smashing little man, a busy little man. He used to have a white coat and a white apron, with a fringe, right down to his ankles. I can see him now, a lovely little chap he was. I used to have to make the invoices out, for people who wanted their orders sent, but if they hadn't paid one week, they didn't get it the next week. Mr Barnet insisted, he said, 'Don't you let anyone have credit: they pay for their goods and then they can have another lot, but not until.' Then we used to have several families used to come in with chits for means test, and they couldn't have butter, and they couldn't have this or that. It used to worry me to death.

It was a lovely old shop. When the war came Percy was on shift work. I had to give up because we never saw each other: he was on night shift and I was on day shift, so I gave up, but I loved it there.

Betty Kyte, born 1919

Horseley Fields

I bought a bungalow at 497 Willenhall Road, but in 1957 my Dad died leaving me to run the family newsagents in Horseley Fields, and the police advised me to live over the shop, because of break-ins, as the area was full of lock-up shops with no one around at night. So I rented out the bungalow.

I well remember all the shops between my bungalow and Piper's Row at the top of Horseley Fields. From the top on the left-hand side there was a bakery, then Wotten's the drapers and Dennison's the butchers. Beyond St James Square there was Machin's, another drapers, then Gough & Loach, then Hawkins' material shop and a household stores selling crockery. Next, past Union Street, was Whitley's, a fried fish shop, Cash Bakery, then the Globe Cinema.

Between Mary Anne Street and St James Street was Hancock's & McCarthy, a jewellers, a hairdressers, Beddows' the greengrocer, a post office and then Jennings, the undertakers. Jennings are the only business still to be found in Horseley Fields from those days, though of course they are in a completely different building.

Next door to the undertakers was St James Church, which I suppose was convenient for funerals, a greengrocers, and then houses as far as the Shakespeare pub at the end of Shakespeare Street. There were factories around Minerva Lane, and the Wulfruna Coal Company by the canal, also still trading – one of the few left in Wolverhampton, I believe, and established in 1850. Beyond that was St Matthew's Church and the Chillington Tool Company.

On the right-hand side of Horseley Fields were the railway offices, then Old Mill Street, leading down to Low Level Station. Next was the Mill pub, then Kitchen's the chemist, Lee's the stationers and newsagent, Wootten's the confectioners and bakers, David's the butchers, just passed Cornhill, then The Two Brothers, who had a large family and made a living as shoe repairers, and Tommy Fullwood's sweet and general store.

Beyond Bradshaw Street was Fishers' dress and shoe shop, the Little Swan pub, where Mr Beards was licensee, then Hollingsworth's the butchers. They did cooked meats and hot faggots and gravy every Friday night. Then there was Deans' cycle shop and the Mount Zion Chapel. That was a beautiful building, with probably about twenty-five steps leading up to the doors. It was said that Mother Shipton, who was reputedly a witch, stood on those steps to foretell the future, hence the name of the next street, Shipton Street, which lead to the canal wharf. This was where barges used to come in before going on to Cadbury's with the crude chocolate. We would go down with the 'blue sugar' bags to get lovely 'raw' chocolate.

Next shops were Smallman's newsagents and tobacconist; Thompkinson's, greengrocers; Sam's, butchers; and Mason's, grocers. After Shipton Street was Fern's, a general store and sweetshop, then the lending library on the

A view looking up Horseley Fields towards the town centre, with Jennings the funeral directors' clock to the left.

The horse-drawn hearses of E.J. Jennings at a much earlier time.

corner of Union Mill Street, with the Union Tap pub on the other corner. After this there was a pet shop, Mrs Lees' general store, Goodall's fried fish shop, James' newsagents, followed by Perry's steel factory and foundry. There were no more shops on that side, though there was the Swan Gardens pub and Willenhall Road School.

Jim Hughes

Warners and Stan Cullis

I started at Warners in 1961 as their stores manager. Before that I was at Cine Equipments in Queen Street, just below and opposite the Express and Star offices. I had started with them about 1953, as their stores manager, then graduated to their chief sales assistant, selling cameras, projectors and everything to do with photography. The Head Office was in Birmingham in Dale End.

I had started work in 1939 at Boulton Paul, which was a bit different, and worked there until 1944 when I was called up. I worked on Defiants and Barracudas at Boulton Paul. I'd had a job lined up in Wolverhampton, at Podmore's, the electricians, but my mother wouldn't let me travel to Wolverhampton; we lived in Codsall at the time. Boulton Paul's was just outside Bilbrook.

Warners was quite a big operation. When I started there they had also got a commercial film department, and they did a lot of work for J.C. Bamford, making commercial films for them. Stan Cullis was one of the directors, and when the managing director, George Dawson, died, Stan, who had then been sacked as manager of the Wolves, became managing director. Truth was he didn't know much about the business; he kept ringing me up and asking me things. One day his secretary rang me up and said Mr Cullis wanted to speak to me, and I said, 'Oh no, not again!'

Then I discovered he was standing right there! I had to say, 'Sorry Mr Cullis.'

Later on he became manager of Birmingham City. He knew a bit more about football than the photography business.

There had been a Mr Warner, which is how they got their name. He started the business off, but with premises below the premises in Chapel Ash. When I was there they had moved and they had two shops, 22 and 26 Chapel Ash. The other was a big audio department, selling recorders and everything to do with audio, and we supplied all the school and education authorities. There was also a commercial photography department.

There was quite a few shops in Chapel Ash then, because before the ring road was built it was only an extension of Darlington Street. Creative Farming were there, and they're still there, but not in the same premises. There was also Hodgetts' paper, tobacco and sweet shop. Later on, Wendy and Tony Hodgetts opened a toy shop further down Chapel Ash, where the art shop is now; he was there for a long while.

The ring road cut off Chapel Ash from the town centre, and a lot of business was lost then. Warners closed the audio shop, and the commercial film department, run by Ken Gamble, closed down; he then started up on his own. The photographic department moved to just off the Bilston Road.

I was at Warners for thirty years until I retired. They were a very good company, and I had a good send-off.

Harry Law, born 1925

Millers toy shop

When I was little, my mother would let me go in Millers, the toy shop in the Central Arcade, but only for two minutes. It was the only thing I liked about shopping in

The Molineux Hotel just before its sad decline into dereliction.

Wolverhampton, though I was impressed by the glass dome in the centre of the arcade, even as a little boy. I expect the Mander Centre would give their eye teeth for an arcade like that now, instead of the concrete tunnels they have. The indoor market was even more impressive, and situated just in the right place, in the heart of the town, instead of the distant corner where it's now located. The first-ever Christmas present I can ever remember buying was in the indoor market; two little brass plates which I had seen my mother admiring. She thought I had bought her the three brass monkeys which I had shown her. 'Hear no evil, see no evil, speak no evil', and I took a childish delight in keeping the secret until Christmas Day.

Woolworth's was also a good place for a little boy to visit. Of course there were two Woolies in Wolverhampton in those day, 'Big Woolies' on the site of the current one, and 'Little Woolies' in Victoria Street, the building now occupied by Barratts of Feckenham. Both Woolies had toys and sweets – what else does a little boy want?

What I cannot understand is that you cannot find anyone in Wolverhampton who remembers the Central Arcade, Queens Arcade and the retail market who does not regret that they were demolished. So if no one in the town wanted it to happen, who was responsible? The same thing applies to the sad decline of the Molineux Hotel and the loss of the beautiful Elephant and Castle pub on Stafford Street. One may be saved but the other is gone for ever.

When I was a boy I used to get taken to see Father Christmas. It was always in Beatties. I don't think he visits there anymore. He didn't so much have a grotto, as an alcove. He

The Elephant and Castle pub on the corner of Stafford Street and the Cannock Road, now demolished.

The author with his baby brother, Peter, meeting Father Christmas in Beatties store in 1953.

would just be sitting there, and you had to go up to him, and he would sit you on his knee and ask what you wanted for Christmas.

I suppose, like a number of people, book-shops are the only shops I regularly visit in the town – sorry, city – centre: W.H. Smith's, which used to be opposite the Grand Theatre until the Mander Centre was built, Beatties book department, Bookland and Waterstones. I learned a little bit about window display at Bookland. When my Albrighton & Shifnal book came out they let me fill one window with vintage agricultural tools and such. The first thing I put in there was a bale of straw, and I suddenly noticed that even when this was the only thing in the window, people were stopping to look, so I quickly put a copy of the book on top of it. They were walking past the other window, which was full of assorted books, without a second glance, and then stopping to look at the straw and the antique tools. I guess if you see something in a window you don't expect, you are more likely to stop and take notice.

Alec Brew, born 1947

Other local titles published by Tempus

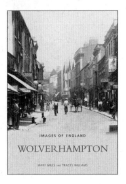

Buildings of Walsall An Illustrated Architectural History
PETER ARNOLD

This book describes and illustrates some of the most historically important architecture to be seen in Walsall today and will serve as a useful guide for those wishing to explore and learn more about the borough's history through its buildings. The New Art Gallery has put Walsall on the UK cultural map, but there are many architectural secrets revealed here by author Peter Arnold, who was Principal Conservation Officer at Walsall Metropolitan Borough Council for thirteen years.
0 7524 2498 X

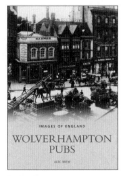

Wolverhampton
MARY MILLS AND TRACEY WILLIAMS

Drawn from the collection held by Wolverhampton Archives and Local Studies, the photographs in this selection recall the changes Wolverhampton underwent between the 1860s and 1960s, a century during which the town centre saw the completion of slum clearance programmes, the building of the ring road, and the construction of two major shopping centres. Also included in this volume are the districts of Finchfield, Whitmore Reans, Parkfields and Blakenhall.
0 7524 3020 3

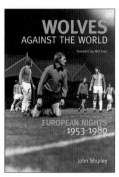

Wolverhampton Pubs
ALEC BREW

This comprehensive volume of archive images recalls the history of many of Wolverhampton's pubs, from the First World War through to the present day. Illustrated with over 200 old photographs and postcards, this collection charts the changing facades of the town's pubs, from street corner pubs like the Hen and Chickens to imposing new pubs built between the wars, such as the Bushbury Arms and the Black Horse. Local characters and lively landlords are also recalled.
0 7524 3156 0

Wolves Against The World
JOHN SHIPLEY

This is the story of those games in the 1950s when Wolves took on the very best teams from around the world, as well as the classic encounters in the European Champions' Cup and European Cup Winners' Cup. Then, in the 1960s, '70s and '80s, it was the turn of the UEFA Cup, Anglo-Italian Cup and Texaco Cup. These were the golden years when football was played at full tilt by the many great international players that have graced Wolves' Molineux stadium.
0 7524 2947 7

If you are interested in purchasing other books published by Tempus, or in case you have difficulty finding any Tempus books in your local bookshop, you can also place orders directly through our website

www.tempus-publishing.com